The Complete Guide to
Using
Depthfinders

Revised Edition

The Complete Guide to Using Depthfinders

Revised Edition

by Buck Taylor

Outdoor Skills Bookshelf
Nashville, Tennessee

ISBN 0-940022-03-6
Library of Congress Catalog Card Number: 84-62198

Printed in the United States of America

This book is dedicated to my Mom and Dad.
God never made better ones.

Contents

Preface   ix

Acknowledgements   xiii

Let Us Begin

   Initial Thoughts on Sonar   **3**

   Depthfinders: How and Why They Work   **8**

      The Basics: What Makes 'em Work?   **12**

      Features and Applications   **16**

Transducer Installation

   The Key to Success   **27**

   "Thru the Hull" Mounting   **33**

   Transom Mounting   **42**

   Finishing the Job Properly   **48**

   Aluminum Hulls: Unanswered Controversy   **53**

   A Second Depthfinder Up Front   **61**

   Concluding Comments   **65**

Operating Procedures

   Basic Operations   **69**

   Miscellaneous Points about Operation   **88**

Signal Interpretation

What the Heck Is *That?*   **97**

    Starting Fresh with Sonar   **98**

    Reading Fish Signals   **105**

Phase Two   **110**

Phase Three   **121**

Time to Go Fishing

Big Bass, Little Bass   **133**

Crappie Any Time You Want Them   **149**

Stripers: The Tackle Busters   **162**

Fun Fish   **180**

Graph Paper Interpretation

More on Reading Graphs   **191**

Winding Up Business

Maintenance Requirements for Sonar   **219**

Troubleshooting on the Water   **236**

Finale   **238**

Appendix   **251**

Credits   **257**

Preface

My own experiences with depthfinders were not very spectacular at first. Actually, I was rather proud just to be able to point out the correct bottom depth to passengers in my boat. Smaller signals which kept appearing on the face of the unit were a mystery, and when questioned about them, I passed them off as "static" or "baitfish." My clients and I also caught a great many treetops in those days while fishing in large schools of bass or crappie which I was "reading" on the depthfinder!

Personally, I have never been a big fan of the "trial-and-error" school for learning. Unfortunately, I was forced to learn about sonar use in exactly that fashion. Years ago, the information on depthfinders which was readily available did little to explain the practical side of fishing with 12 volts. Papers which came in the box with depthfinders in those days pretty much limited their instructional value to the basics of seeing the bottom and a few mid-range images.

As manufacturers began making advances in both technology and product quality, it became increasingly evident there was a great deal of very valuable information to be gained by using sonar properly when fishing. I wrote for freebie handout material, searching everywhere for anything practical to read on sonar. Other fishermen were questioned eagerly, and each time I discovered something new, I logged it into a notebook. This went on for a couple of years. My ability to use depthfinders successfully on the lake for fishing increased materially.

About that time I negotiated the job of writing a five-feature series of articles on depthfinders for a national magazine. The challenge was interesting, but the research requirements would be awesome. Deciding it might be fun to increase my own knowledge about sonar while taking a few bucks from the publisher, I started work. At the time I had no idea the hours spent and dollars required in expenses would result in a financial disaster before the deal was finished. It took over 12 months.

I had leaned very heavily upon the technical staffs of several leading depthfinder manufacturers; had found and interviewed several genuine experts on the subject of sonar use; and had amassed enough notes, tapes, illustrations and related material to fill an average living room, floor to ceiling. Then the letters started pouring in.

I got rave reviews from the sonar authorities and letters of appreciation from fishermen who said they had finally found something in print that was genuinely helpful on the subject. People wrote from almost every state in the U.S., and even from a few foreign countries. One fisherman in South Africa wrote to say his angling pals considered depthfinders to present an "unfair advantage" for the fisherman. His was one of the letters I answered personally.

The magazine elected to use only a fraction of the material I had gathered, insisting they also have other articles and advertisements in each issue. Rather proud of my research and the reader responses coming in, I decided to write a full-length book on how to use depthfinders effectively. It was a success, selling in all 50 states and 18 foreign countries over the next four years.

Yet, during those four years the technology used in building depthfinders advanced so much it became necessary to update the text. Thus this Revised Edition. Initially, again digging into research on the new machines, I was practically overcome with fancy computer lingo used to describe "state of the art" goodies. The video units were in a class by themselves, and the improved paper graph units used electronics which could rival the special effects in *Star Wars*.

Fortunately, after many hours of study I realized the basic principles actually had not changed much. There is an infinite amount of gingerbread available on the units today, and when you buy one of the really fancy depthfinders, you'll be able to perform extremely sophisticated maneuvers searching for fish. But down-to-earth facts on depthfinder usage are pretty much the same today as they were a few years back, and should remain so.

Taking that approach, I have revised this book to include some of the newer features available, but have tried to state clearly the things you truly must know in using your sonar machine with maximum efficiency. You are about to learn in rapid fashion all the information it took years for me to understand.

My goal is to help you save a similar number of years trying to figure out what all that stuff you see on a depthfinder dial, chart or screen really means.

Buck Taylor

Acknowledgements

The author wishes to express his thanks and appreciation to the following individuals who contributed, in a variety of ways, to the research and production of this book:

Charlie Brewer
CRAZY HEAD TACKLE COMPANY

Larry Colombo
TECHSONIC INDUSTRIES, INC.

Ted Hansford
SMITH'S INDUSTRIES, INC.

Thayne Smith
LOWRANCE ELECTRONICS, INC.

A very special word of appreciation goes to my wife, Martha, whose contribution to my well-being began the day we met and has never slowed.

The Complete Guide to
Using
Depthfinders

Revised Edition

1

Let Us Begin

Initial Thoughts on Sonar

The mere presence of a depthfinder in your boat will not cause fish to jump over the sides to land in your live-well or ice chest. In addition, the act of turning on your unit will not automatically cause fish to gather in mass below the boat. Depthfinders do not create hunger pains in fish, either. As if these bothersome thoughts were not enough to make your wallet tremble while checking out the price tag on modern sonar gear, there is more.

A few American anglers still continue to catch fish without use of sonar equipment at all. In at least one extreme case, I know a bank executive who has been exposed to all the heavy-duty operational niceties of multiple-unit sonar gear in my boat, and he still insists he can catch as many, if not more, fish without depthfinders than I can while using mine. A point, you may wish to note, which he gleefully has proven on more than one occasion.

Having now given credit to my banker, I shall make an attempt to justify the bucks you have spent, or are about to

spend, on depthfinders. In all honesty, the use of sonar gear must be done with an eye for moderation. There is little cost-effectiveness in bolting a $1,200 graph unit on the bench seat of your 10-foot johnboat. The unit will be capable of performing a number of feats under water conditions unlikely to be experienced by typical johnboat users who rarely venture far from shore. Yet you will be forced to pay for the numerous dials, knobs, whistles, and gingerbread built into the expensive graph, even though you never use them. It is purchases of that nature which always lead to "peace offerings" at home. Gifts to one's spouse on the heels of purchasing an expensive sonar unit are part of the cause for the ever-increasing cost of fishing today.

Matching sonar equipment to the fishing conditions you will encounter is only logical. If your pleasure consists mainly of capturing fillets in water of 30-foot depths or less, you have small need for units capable of drawing out Ice Age remnants on the ocean floor. A simple flasher unit with a 50-foot scale will do nicely, thank you.

Conversely, if you love fishing for the big stripers that cruise deep, open waters in man-made reservoirs, you will need a more sophisticated sonar tool. When the bottom depth exceeds the maximum depth shown on the depthfinder scale, funny things happen. On a graph, you simply watch the bottom disappear from sight on the paper, to be drawn in at some imaginary point down around your shoelaces. When bottom gets too deep for a flasher, it starts giving you fake readings; the bottom signals continue on around the face of the dial to appear somewhere else which seems appropriate to the unit.

Deep-water sonar requirements can be met in a number of ways. You can purchase units with 100-foot depth scales or even more. You can purchase a unit with multiple scales,

allowing you to shift gears with the flick of a switch, trans-
forming the depth readout from one set of numbers to
another. In the event of an emergency (either financial or
unexpected water depth), you can watch the signals carefully on your flasher as they make a complete circle around
the dial. If your flasher has a 60-foot depth scale and the
water is 85 feet deep, the bottom reading on the unit will
make a complete circle around the dial, pass "0" and stop
to rest at "25 feet" on the scale.

    While this is all very logical to your sonar flasher, it
requires that you notice when the bottom reading sneaks
past the "0" reading. Then it becomes a simple matter to
add two figures together to find the correct bottom depth. If

This SI-TEX FL-8 flasher offers four depth ranges, displays returning signals in three colors.

the flasher shows bottom at 25 feet after passing the "0" point, you add the maximum depth on the dial (30, 50, 60 feet, etc.) to discover where the world is under the boat. In the case of a 60-foot flasher, you would probably calculate bottom at 60 + 25, the sum of which is usually 85.

In my younger days I had a souped-up Chevy with a 454 engine and a speedometer which read only up to 100 mph. On the drag strip I was faced with the same situation mentioned above, the speedometer needle passing the "maximum" speed and continuing on around to start again. As the rather powerful engine would roar to 120 mph in

second gear, it was an every-weekend affair to watch the
needle make a full circle, pass the blank area where there
were no numbers, and climb to 30 or 40 mph again. However, unlike the sonar flasher's signal, I rarely failed to
know when this was taking place.

Selecting the proper sonar unit for your personal type
of fishing activity is quite important, financially and func-
tionally. A clear idea of how sonar really works will prove
helpful in the selection.

Depthfinders:
How and Why They Work

Once used mostly for military chores like detecting
underwater reefs and enemy vessels, sonar (SOund NAvigation Ranging) today helps fishermen fill stringers, win tournaments and keep their boats away from places hazardous to
the health of props, lower units and fiberglass hulls. There
are literally dozens of depthfinder models on the market at
present, and all work in a similar fashion using the principles of sonar. Unit features, quality and capabilities vary
substantially, as do price tags. Yet below the cosmetics,
there lies a pulsating heart of crystal which can be the most
important tool in your boat when fish are playing hard to
find.

One does not have to understand complex formulas,
nor have graduated from technical school with honors to use
sonar equipment properly. Neither is it required that you
know each piece of circuitry within the unit by name and
color code. If that were the case, you may rest assured I
would not be writing this book. And chances are pretty good
you would not be reading it, either.

Yet the complexities are all there to serve you. Some units have self-adjusting, practically "hands off" operation to compensate for water depth changes. Others offer dual-frequency transducers providing appropriate performance for either shallow or very deep use. You can even link some models with a Loran-C unit to have your exact coordinates printed out right on the chart paper!

Microprocessor circuitry produces Space Age technology which allows you to examine only a "slice" or layer of the water at a time, even zoom the detail within a given sector into still larger, more detailed displays. These mini-computers have noise reject features to block electrical interference and/or eliminate "cross talk" between two separate units running in the same boat. The really fancy ones can actually eliminate most of the surface clutter by varying the sensitivity level in the receiver for close (surface) signals and more distant (fish, structure) signals.

Digital units are not discussed in this book. They are great for navigation and for getting a true bottom reading. The better ones are guaranteed not to find fish.

Video depthfinders, whether considered "fad" or "state of the art," are the industry's attempt to bridge the gap between flashers and graphs. They display images on a screen instead of burning them on paper, some store the most-recent info for recall, and many can be stopped or "frozen" for study. With dual-angle transducers, dual-frequency transmitters and the ability to vary the pulse length on transmission, there is virtually no combination the average fisherman is likely to encounter that modern depthfinders cannot handle. But as mentioned in the Preface, I'm going to explain the ways to *use* your depthfinder effectively, not bore you with technicalities.

Properly installed and operated, a good depthfinder will furnish a staggering amount of useful information for the person who takes time in learning how to read the signals. Indeed, there is an initial time period when serious study must be given to understanding sonar readout. You cannot simply bolt one of the things onto your boat and flip on the switch expecting the fun to materialize as if by magic. Learning takes time. *Lots of time* in the case of depthfinders. You may well read this book three or four times before everything I am going to tell you comes true in the real world where you fish. But when it all falls into place for you finally, your success on the water is going to increase dramatically. That much I can promise in return for the 10 bucks you spent here.

Credit: Lowrance Electronics, Inc.

The Lowrance System 2000 flashers offer multiple depth ranges and short pulse lengths for better resolution.

Many depthfinders have special features designed to assist in particular fishing procedures. Some, for example, are excellent for reading details in very deep water. Others work far more efficiently in shallow areas. Many graphs and flashers have selective depth scales built into their operational systems which allow a full range of detailed readout in a variety of water depths. For the most part, it will be your personal ability to understand what the unit is saying, rather than the fancy stuff the salesman liked, that enables you to put fillets on the supper table. After analyzing your needs from sonar, you will be in a better position to evaluate the features offered on units you may view in the store.

The Basics: What Makes 'em Work?

There are three fundamental parts to your sonar system. When you add electricity, they work together to generate the desired result: the image on a screen or dial which details shapes and objects in the water beneath your boat.

1—*The Transmitter.* A small amount of current from your battery is taken by the transmitter and converted into pulses. These pulses are then fed to the transducer which is in the water.

2—*The Transducer.* As the pulses from the transmitter reach the transducer, they are modified, making a complete change from electrical impulses to sound impulses. These mechanical sound waves are then released into the water from the transducer "eye," or the center of its internal crystal.

Sound pulses travel away from the transducer at just under 5,000 feet per second in the water. When they strike an underwater object (fish, treetops, bottom, etc.) they are bounced, or reflected back up to the waiting transducer. Called "echoes" after striking something below, the reflected sound waves again enter the transducer where they are converted back into electrical impulses.

3—*The Receiver.* The returning echoes, once converted back into electrical form, are run through an amplifier to boost their weakened condition from the trip. They are then used to display information on the face of your unit. A perfectly-synchronized, spinning wheel or belt beneath the dial uses these tiny bursts of electricity to either light a neon bulb (flasher units), or flow through the tip of a keen wire stylus moving across the face of treated paper (graph units).

Flashers light up and graphs burn marks on paper with the returning electrical pulses. (Video units don't need belts or wheels, merely displaying signals directly on the screen.)

As the speed of sound traveling through water is known and remains constant, the depthfinder can give accurate readings for distance to the object reflecting the signal, based upon the time required for the energy pulse to make the complete trip out and back. The spinning wheel or belt revolves at exactly the speed necessary for it to be in the correct position on the depth scale when the returning signal is received, converted and fed to the bulb or stylus. Nowhere is the phrase "timing is everything" more appropriate than when applied to the inner workings of your depthfinder.

You might look at the face of your unit and think the readings are constant, especially at the "0" mark on the dial. Actually, your unit is sending out pulses one at a time. Each and every pulse must be sent and received back before the next one can begin the trip. This is why the belt or wheel on your depthfinder slows noticeably when you change over to a deeper depth scale. The unit actually gears itself down to a pace slow enough to insure it can capture the returning pulse from the maximum depth on the scale you are using before sending out another one.

A typical sounding rate for flashers may be 24 times per second, while some specialty graphs may have a rate slowed to only once every two seconds.

According to the experts, the exact type power supplied to the depthfinder is not keenly important. Almost all depthfinders today work on 12-volt DC current, and the differences between wet-cell batteries and those with dry

Credit: Tennessee Wildlife Resources Agency

cells have little or no effect on performance. The wet-cell battery normally lasts a little longer in practice, but depthfinders are designed to use only the correct amount of current required. You will not get more power to the unit by using a wet-cell over a dry-cell battery. In fact, you can operate the depthfinder perfectly by taking a pair of six-volt lantern batteries and wiring them in series.

There is no question that your depthfinder should be fired by the main battery in your boat *if* the only alternative is the battery which operates the trolling motor. Your engine constantly recharges the main battery while running, providing a steady voltage level. Operated from the trolling motor battery, current to the depthfinder will get weaker and weaker as the day progresses. The *depthfinder* will not weaken the battery materially in a month of use. But the trolling motor will do it routinely in a matter of a few hours work.

Depthfinders draw very little current, but like a finely-tuned carburetor in the Indy 500, they need their juice full

strength to operate at maximum performance levels. When
your battery begins to weaken, it cannot provide a full dose
of energy to the depthfinder, and the results suffer. You
might compare the situation to having an all-night date with
Dolly Parton after spending the afternoon with the Mandrell
sisters.

Features and Applications

Special Scales or Depth Readings. Should your fishing
activities be confined to water 20 feet or less in depth the
year around, the value of having multiple depth scales on
your unit would hold little importance. You could select a
unit giving maximum detail for the "0 to 20-foot" band of
water, and have everything you need in the way of sonar
readout. But if you should take that limited unit into water
of say 50 or 100-foot depth in search of a few stripers for
supper, the signals would be almost impossible to read.

A depthfinder with a single, 50-foot depth scale will
show bottom readings accurately at 65 feet (or any other
reasonable depth). However, as mentioned earlier, the
"bottom" reading will appear on the unit at 15 feet. Should
you be searching for suspended fish holding at 10 or 20 feet
over the deeper water, you would have a tough time trying
to sort out fish signals from bottom signals on the dial. This
is where selective depth scales are big medicine for fishermen. Flip the switch, and you can alter the maximum depth
reading to double or triple the original scale on the dial.

Incidentally, running over 55-foot water while watching a depthfinder set on the 50-foot scale can lead to coronary problems if your boat is booming along at 50 or 60
mph!

On graph units, it frequently works much to your ad-

Credit: Tennessee Wildlife Resources Agency

vantage in having the ability to *reduce* the depth scale. By doing so, you can utilize the full width of the paper, and display details in larger, easier-to-read fashion. Some modern depthfinder manufacturers offer graphs with depth scales as shallow as "0 to 12 feet." With detail like that available on paper, you should be able to spot with ease the differences between Neptune and his mermaids.

Signal Cones. Researching material from a number of sonar manufacturers, I found a wide range of cone angles in their transducers. The cone angle basically translates into the shape of the sound pulses in the water after they leave your transducer. The pulses begin at the eye of the transducer and spread in an ever-increasing circle as they get

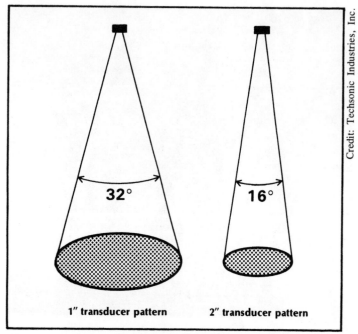

32°   **16°**

1″ transducer pattern   **2″ transducer pattern**

Transducer Patterns

further away. The "degree" of cone angle simply means how fast or how slow the pulses spread. It's a rather complex subject and involves a good bit of theoretical thinking. One manufacturer told me that the angle of the cone is a product of the inverse relationship between the diameter of the crystal and the energy which passes through it. Whatever the heck that means.

Anyway, some cone angles are as tight as eight degrees, while others are wide enough to reach 50 degrees. The difference in square footage of underwater real estate represented by the returning signals in these cases is quite substantial. A "wide" cone angle will show you the treetop and the fish playing cards next to it. A narrow cone angle may only show you the Red Ace.

On the subject of cone angles, manufacturers are not likely to agree. The guy whose inverse whatchacallit makes a tight cone says he has concentrated the power into a smaller area, and his unit produces superior detail in that area of readout. Then the other guy whose machine displays detail over a wider bottom area will counter by saying he gives you a better idea of what is really under the boat, instead of providing only a peek at little pieces of H_2O. Within reason, both are correct.

Just for comparison purposes, a transducer shooting a 22-degree cone into water which is 20 feet deep, would produce readout detail on an area of the bottom having an eight-foot diameter. Another unit sporting an eight-degree cone would produce activity reports over a bottom circle with a three-foot diameter at the same depth. Perhaps a fair comparison of the two would be to think about the differences between a floodlight matched against a spotlight, if the power source remains constant. Which would you rather have when walking through a swamp filled with alligators?

Transducer Frequencies. Apparently, each sonar manufacturer fine tunes the frequency of his units slightly differently. Lowrance is at 192 kHz, Humminbird is at 200 kHz, and so forth. Other common frequencies range from 38 to 150 kHz; however, most of the units suitable for freshwater fishing today are in the higher ranges. *Lower* frequencies in depthfinders have less power loss, making them ideal for very deep water. The *higher* frequencies with shorter pulse lengths are much better suited to giving fine detail in the readout.

Superior detail-producing ability is called *resolution*.

Some of the high-frequency kHz units on the market today can isolate, or separate, a fish holding only a few inches from the bottom. These same units can draw the thermocline layer in the water on your graph paper because of the sudden temperature change, which also causes a change in water density. Such is the world of high-frequency units.

Unfortunately, nothing in this world is perfect. High-frequency sonar units do not perform well in extremely deep water. The signals are absorbed somewhat by the objects they strike. The problem is relatively small in waters most freshwater anglers are likely to fish, but saltwater captains who fish the briny depths probably wouldn't trade you a rusty hook for a dozen high-frequency units if they had to use them.

Portable Units. Several manufacturers presently offer units with bolt-on or suction cup transducer mounts. These portable depthfinders normally feature self-contained batteries and are a favorite with many anglers who do not have their own boats. Portability is a great advantage to the fisherman on vacation who must rent a boat, or one who fishes upon occasion with a pal whose rig lacks sonar advantages.

Whiteline, Grayline Feature. Many quality graphs offer a feature which enables the operator to ''lift'' objects away from the bottom reading on the paper. The feature does not actually increase the distance between the bottom and nearby objects. It shades out the heavy bottom reading so that objects near it will blend less. This makes it much easier to spot fish lying close to the bottom. Without the feature, fish signals often tend to blend into the bottom reading and go unseen. I think the majority of the better graph units on the market today offer this feature. It definitely is worth asking for when shopping.

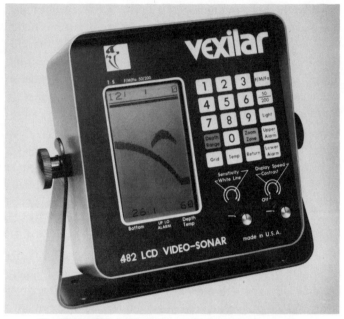

Vexilar's 482 LCD Video unit features "zoom"
ability, dual-frequency selection (50 kHz or
200 kHz), display in feet, meters or fathoms, speed
and temperature.

Dual-color Signals. Unique in the industry as far as I
know, SI-TEX has marketed a flasher unit which displays
the bottom reading in red and fish signals in yellow. I
haven't the slightest idea how it works, but it does. It will
not show different colors for fish holding inside the confines
of a treetop, nor for fish spending the day on the bottom.

Chart Paper Retainer. This feature has real advantages
for the serious fisherman who saves his chart paper for
future reference. Some graphs spew out the used paper to
flap in the wind or be torn off at regular intervals when it

becomes a nuisance. The retainer incorporates a take-up spool which captures the used paper neatly.

Serious fishermen often take notes of conditions and results of their efforts on the graph paper as the action takes place. Date, time of day, location, etc., can all be jotted down in code on the chart paper, generating a permanent record for future use in duplicating the fun. These notes then become a valuable record regarding patterns and techniques which proved successful on a particular lake at a given time and circumstance. Retaining the well-documented chart paper can prove important when you fish the same area the following year, or even the next day.

Transducer Switch-over Box. You can purchase a

Credit: Joel Arrington

switch box which allows the boat operator to use either of two transducers for the same depthfinder. The advantages are numerous with this set-up; perhaps the most important is that it saves you from having to buy a second unit under some conditions. One transducer might be mounted in the rear of the boat for use while cruising slowly in search of fish and structure. The second transducer could be mounted on the foot of your trolling motor for use when it's time to get serious about the whole deal. You can use the switch box to change over from one transducer to the other any time you choose. In addition to granting multiple use from a single unit, the dual transducer routine can be valuable when trying to work out a narrow creek channel or a long, slender underwater point. The 10 to 16-foot spread between readings can be a big help when trying to stay on target. Using this accessory, you can place the depthfinder on a swivel mount and read it from any direction in the boat. Buying two transducers is cheaper on the family finances than buying a pair of units.

Summary. This covers the basics of how sonar works and why it tells you the distance between your transducer and various underwater objects. We might close out this chapter with two simple statements:

1—Don't purchase a new sonar unit which has features you will never use unless they come as standard equipment on the unit which best fits your needs.

2—There is nothing in the Wonderful World of Sonar which allows a manufacturer to produce depthfinders at drastically reduced prices, yet maintain comparable quality with the more expensive models.

2

Transducer Installation

The Key to Success

In a series of articles I did for *Bassmaster Magazine* on depthfinders, I titled the one on transducers as "The Weakest Link." It was an appropriate tag to hang on the discussion. In my honest opinion, about one-half of the transducers being used by fishermen today probably are not installed and/or maintained properly to produce optimum performance. And my opinion is backed by several experts in the sonar business.

Service repair shops, both factory-operated and independent, say a healthy percentage of complaints from depthfinder owners about their unit's performance can be traced directly back to poor transducer installation. It might be worth noting that the units returned for service obviously came from people who were having *severe problems and knew it!* There is no way to guess how many others are having only slightly less-severe problems and don't fully realize what's happening (and not happening) with their unit's performance.

Proper installation of your transducer is keenly
important. Be sure to read the instructions for
installation which come with the unit.

Transducer installation is a bit like tying on the lure
before casting into a splashing, feeding school of fish. You
know the knot is important, but you get in a big hurry to
enjoy the fun which is coming up next. Maybe the average
fisherman is so anxious to get on the water that he overlooks
the critical importance of proper transducer installation.
Maybe he doesn't read the manual carefully (if he kept it at

all). In either event, poor installation of his transducer instantly becomes a weak link in the system.

The sonar equipment you try so carefully to read on the water cannot produce truly meaningful information if the transducer is poorly installed. It's that basic. The importance of correct procedures in the location and physical installation of your depthfinder transducer cannot be overemphasized. It makes no difference what brand sonar machine you have.

Transducers:
What They Can and Cannot Do

Transducers are designed to fire a signal through the water, then receive it back after that signal strikes something and bounces, or reflects, back upward. "Through the water" is the critical part of that description. *Transducers cannot shoot (or receive) signals through the air.*

The entire matter of transducer operation is very simple. You put it under the surface of the water, point it at the bottom, and it works. I have found schools of fish, treetops and various structures on my sonar unit by simply holding the transducer over the side of the boat in my hand. Simple. You can tape the pod to a broom handle or a canoe paddle, stick it beneath the surface and get good readout on your depthfinder. So why all the fuss?

Aside from getting cramps in your wrist from holding a transducer overboard, you soon discover that boat movement causes a problem. As most of us like to use sonar for finding fish while we cruise along searching for them in a moving boat, it evolves that the transducer must be mounted somehow to keep it in position. In most instances, success-

Credit: Vexilar, Inc.

Standard Transducer

ful mounting depends upon the boat speed you desire while operating the depthfinder.

For example, portable depthfinders usually come with the transducer mounted on a metal rod (or a rubber suction cup), and the rod has clamps to use in attaching it to the boat gunwale. While a good deal more sophisticated, this set-up is similar to taping the puck on a broom handle and sticking it into the water. At *very* slow speeds, the rod and transducer can remain in the water, continuing to work just fine. But as boat speed increases, air bubbles begin to churn around the transducer, causing poor readings. And if the

The "Tom Mann Bird Trap" from Humminbird adapts
to hold flasher units in a self-contained,
portable fashion.

speed increases slightly more, you'll find the rod bent or snatched out of its bracket.

Mounting the transducer on the foot of your electric trolling motor is an excellent choice for slow-motion fish hunting. The trolling motor is used to ease the boat along, and the transducer remains totally submerged. Trolling motor speed will not cause air bubbles to form on the pod (usually strapped to the motor housing with oversize radiator hose clamps). The depthfinder and trolling motor

electrical systems do not fight each other, so you have a very workable situation with this mounting location.

But you still don't have cruising speed in the boat while the depthfinder is in use.

This is where things begin to get tricky. You can mount the transducer inside the boat, shooting signals through the hull, or you can bolt it on the outside bottom of the transom beneath the water level. Generally speaking, either of the two mountings will allow for medium-to-high-speed readings while the boat is underway. For this reason, most fishermen will opt for one of these procedures. Aluminum boats present a few special considerations for transducer mounting, as you will see shortly.

"Thru the Hull" Mounting

The term can be taken two ways. There are transducers on the market today which are mounted by drilling a hole completely through the hull. A long, threaded shaft extends from the transducer, and this shaft is poked up through the hull where it is secured by washers and a big bolt. Epoxy, waterproof caulking and regular church attendance prevent the mount from leaking. The transducer itself remains in the water, snugged tightly to the outside of the hull. On some boats, especially the larger ones, this mounting is outstanding in performance. Big boats rarely go rocketing over stump rows.

More commonly, "Thru the Hull" mounting means affixing the transducer to a suitable spot inside the boat, and shooting the *signals* through the hull into the water. The advantages of this mounting procedure are numerous.

Shooting signals through the hull will:

- Eliminate the chance of damage to the transducer if you run over a log or water buffalo.
- Allow for maximum high-speed readings.
- Prevent algae or oil build-up on the eye of the transducer.
- Prevent accidental damage to your transducer while trailering your rig in a crosswind.
- Eliminate the need for drilling holes in the transom beneath the water line.
- Solve a few problems with electrical interference from your big engine (maybe).

Many fiberglass boat builders provide a special cut-out in the rear one-third of the boat, designated as the optimum location for interior mounting of your transducer. Depending upon the expertise in these matters which the manufac-

Strips of plywood are used for reinforcement strength in many fiberglass boat hulls. Your transducer cannot shoot signals through these wooden obstacles.

*The Eagle Silent Thirty II is a computer-controlled
flasher with two depth ranges.*

turer has, the pre-determined location is usually the best
choice. It may be the *only* spot on that hull where you can
easily mount your transducer.

The 1978 Flotation Law which the U.S. Coast Guard
presented to boat manufacturers has made it necessary to
have a certain amount of foam flotation material placed
permanently into most boats under 20 feet in length. Frequently, this foam is positioned next to the hull beneath the
floor, and has a way of being needed most in exactly the
spot where you wish to put the transducer. Transducers
cannot shoot a signal through foam.

Along similar lines, product liability insurance costs

have caused many manufacturers to beef up the structural integrity of their boat hulls. This has resulted in things like having strips of plywood glassed into the hull in the rear one-third of the boat, use of false floors with air space between the hull and deck, and the construction technique of using a balsa wood layer joined to the hull over all or part of the inner surface. As you might expect, transducers cannot shoot signals through any of that stuff, either.

Faced with a fiberglass boat lacking a factory cut-out for mounting your transducer, and finding your boat has any of the above construction techniques for added strength in the hull, you have a decision facing you. You can cut, drill and cuss your way thru the foam and flooring until you reach the thin glass shell, or you can hang the transducer off the transom. If you elect to chop out your own mounting spot, you must continue your labors until reaching the raw fiberglass hull. Going too far with the blade will puncture the hull; stopping short of the raw glass will leave signal-deadening material between your transducer and the optimum readings you want.

If you *really* want to mount the thing inside the boat and refuse to consider mounting it on the transom, you would be smart to pay the factory people to handle this little chore for you. (This is especially true, because at this point, you ain't exactly sure where the optimum location is, anyway!) And like bets on a horse after the window closes, once the deed is done, it's too late to change your mind!

Fortunately or unfortunately (I'm not sure which), all glass boats do not have this layer of foam and/or wood in the back end. If your boat has the factory location spelled out for you, mount the transducer there and hope they had it figured out correctly. If there is no set spot designated, and you find an area where the basic hull is accessible, you'll

have to do a bit of experimenting before selecting the final resting place for your transducer.

Clean out the sump area diligently with warm, soapy water. I realize this procedure often requires one to perform the activity in an inverted position, but bite the bullet and do a good job. You'll only have to do this once per boat.

Drain the water; rinse out the area well. Refill the sump with fresh water to a depth of perhaps two inches. Go to the lake and have a pal drive the boat for you C – A – R – E – F – U – L – L – Y while you peer over the transom. If you are positive your marriage is secure, you might request your spouse serve as the driver. If not, this operation might be best accomplished on an area of the lake which enjoys little or no sun-bathing activity by local beauties, the same being

*SI-TEX HE-203 provides five ranges with zoom
ability, two different pulse lengths, blocks out
interference.*

a definite distraction to the average boat driver. In any
event, peer over the transom while the boat is being run at
perhaps half-throttle or slightly better. Observe the location
on the transom which experiences the least amount of turbulence coming from underneath while underway. Mark the
spot.

Next, park and anchor the boat over a drop-off or some
underwater trees in about 30-foot water. The structure can
be found easily enough by holding the transducer in your
hand for a bit of searching and coasting. When the boat is
resting still, turn the depthfinder on full power; i.e., crank
the sensitivity knob wide open. You are now ready to discover the optimum spot in the sump for mounting your
transducer.

The water in the sump will provide good contact between the transducer and the hull. Rub away any air bubbles which may form on the two surfaces. With the depthfinder running, move the puck around on the hull in the immediate vicinity of your mark indicating smooth water under the transom. When you find the spot which appears to give the best readings on the face of your depthfinder, mark it well. (Scratch an "x" with your pocket knife, etc.) Now, you must test the location further.

Again, holding the transducer in your hand, place it over the side and beneath the water surface completely. Compare the detail shown on your depthfinder while hand-holding the pod, with the detail you observed when shooting signals through the hull. As you are looking at the identical structure below while the boat remains stationary, a major difference in the two readings can only mean you have a subfloor, foam or something else beneath the sump. Yep. That means you have a problem. If subsequent experiments do not reveal a location in the sump which provides comparable detail with the hand-held readings, you must either cut through the subfloor or mount the transducer on the transom.

On the brighter side, if you find only minor differences between the two readings, you're in business. Go home and finish the job. A tiny snort of man's best friend may be in order after the boat is on the trailer.

Drain and dry the bilge (sump) area. Sandpaper the selected location for mounting. Sandpaper right down to the raw fiberglass. Remove dust and debris from the location after you finish. Be sure there are no paint chips or other foreign matter in the circle you just made with the sander.

Some manufacturers recommend building a small dam or enclosure around the mounting location. This is suggested to prevent having the securing agent (usually

Credit: Joel Arrington

epoxy cement) from running. It's a good idea. You can also reduce the problem by insuring the boat (trailer) is quite level prior to the activity.

Experts advise you to use a two-part epoxy cement for securing the transducer to the hull. None that I know will recommend the use of silicone, because it seems to remain

Credit: Ray Jefferson

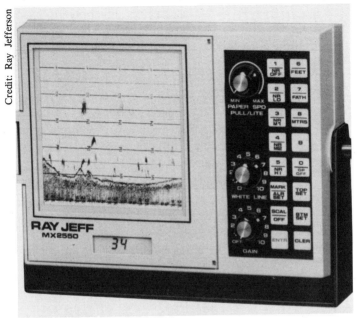

Ray Jeff MX-2550 has a LCD reading down to 2,500 feet, uses micro-processor circuitry to zoom detail.

as a gel beneath the pod for quite some time, and that can reduce the sensitivity of readings. Silicone also is affected by oil and gas spills, which eventually ruin the installation.

Select a two-part epoxy with a fairly long drying time. The 30-minute variety is better than the five-minute variety. The reason for this choice hinges upon the fact that fast-curing epoxy has a tendency to generate heat while it cures. The heat can cause air bubbles to form, and by now, you should know air bubbles on or under the transducer create a definite "no-no" for optimum performance.

Mix the epoxy *slowly* and *carefully* in a container. Do

not whip the mixture enthusiastically, as this only produces air bubbles in the mess. Place a coating of epoxy on the face of the transducer and set it aside. Pour the remaining cement onto the location for mounting. It is not necessary, but you can take a hair dryer to heat the epoxy for *only a few seconds,* which thins the mixture slightly and will further eliminate the formation of air bubbles.

Place the transducer face into position, push down firmly and work it gently to force out air and excess cement. It is keenly important that you not leave air beneath the puck. Once the transducer is in position, place a weight on top of it to hold it there securely. Leave it alone for several hours, and don't let the kids play in your boat while the epoxy is drying.

Transom Mounting

Procedures and "angle of attack" vary from one manufacturer to the next, but the instruction manual which comes with your depthfinder generally does a good job explaining the proper installation method for transom mounting. There is little to be gained here by repeating all that verbage because you can read it for free from the box your sonar unit came in. However, there are some tips worth mentioning on the procedure, and these do not appear in most instruction manuals.

Mounting your transducer on the boat transom will:
- Provide the easiest and fastest method of installation which allows accurate readings at cruising speeds.
- Increase the chance of damage to the transducer by striking foreign objects in the water.

Credit: Tennessee Wildlife Resources Agency

- Offer a mounting system which is easily changed.
- Allow you to swap transducers any time you choose.
- Demand more attention to maintenance of the

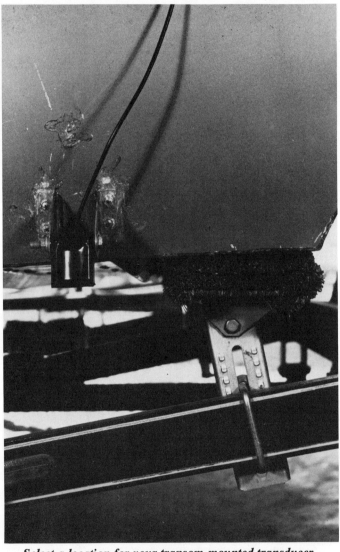

Select a location for your transom-mounted transducer which will not interfere with trailering the boat.

transducer than interior mounting does.
- Require closer attention to water turbulence caused by slight irregularities in installation.

The procedure for mounting your transducer on the transom begins with the same "looking over the transom while running" procedure as described above. Check for an area under the transom which shows the least amount of water turbulence while the boat is chugging along at half or three-quarters speed. In the case of transom mounting, I suggest you mark *two* places which show the most smooth water. This allows you to examine the choice spots later when the boat is sitting on your trailer.

They say "Experience is the name by which we call our own mistakes." You might as well benefit from my experience. I recommend you mark a pair of smooth-water locations on the transom for two reasons: 1) After the boat is sitting on your trailer, you can check to see if placing a transducer in either location will interfere with the act of trailering the boat, or if having a transducer there will make it nervous because of the bunks or carpeted runners on the trailer itself. 2) In the case of an aluminum boat, you can decide which location has the least number of rivets and hull irregularities in front of it by examining the next six or eight feet of tin ahead of the transom. It is quite possible the hull irregularities you discover were not creating excessive turbulence because of the particular speed the boat was traveling when you made your observation. Believe me, a faster or slower speed could change the whole ball game.

Choose the location which offers the greatest ease in trailering the boat, and which features the most smooth hull configuration forward of the spot.

As the transom mount will position the transducer below the water level with nothing between it and the hard

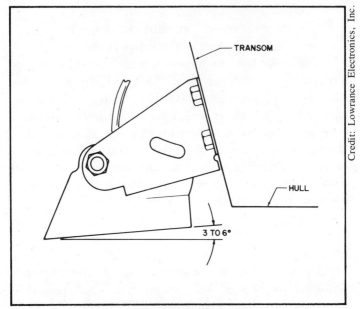

Credit: Lowrance Electronics, Inc.

Transom Mount – Point Forward
Side View

world except water, you can bypass the exercise of comparing readings between hand-held signals and potential-
location signals. Once the decision has been made on the
best spot for installation, you might as well take a deep
breath and start drilling holes in your boat.

    Most problems with transom mounts come from either
the lack of a smooth joining between transducer and hull, or
an improper angle on the transducer face. Many pilgrims try
to put the face of the transducer exactly flush with the bottom of the boat, but they leave a gap between where the boat
ends and the transducer begins. The gap simply allows
water to swirl around in the space, creating turbulence that

wasn't there before. A painfully-smoothed-over "bridge" of silicone between the two surfaces can eliminate the problem. Don't get silicone on the face of the transducer.

Some transom-mounted transducers work far better if they are dropped well below the hull level. This allows the thing to cut its own way thru the water without regard to what is happening a half-inch above its smooth, pointed nose. The risk of smacking it with a log is greatly increased, but usually, so is the performance.

That "angle of attack" business means only the amount of tilt you give the face of the transducer in the water. The recommended angle is provided in the instructions, although most folks cannot recognize a six–degree angle any quicker than I can. Here again, experiment a bit on the water until you find the best angle for yourself, then use lock washers and a little muscle to keep the transducer in that position.

For those who don't like to get their feet wet, I suggest putting a liberal amount of silicone sealer in and around the holes you are required to drill in the transom to mount the bracket(s). Again speaking from my "experience," you will find that time given to marking the holes for the bracket neatly and accurately will prevent all sorts of problems, not the least of which is having three screw holes close together which combine in a single hole large enough to stick your little finger into.

Finally, bumps on the road while trailering, and pressures from the water while running, can eventually change the "angle of attack" on the transom-mounted transducer if the bolts and washers securing same are not tight. Changing the tilt on the puck can cause poor performance in the readout, so you are required to check this situation frequently during the season.

Finishing the Job Properly

Transducer properly in place securely, either inside the boat or on the transom, there still remain a few tasks to accomplish before dashing to the lake. The depthfinder itself must be mounted somewhere, and the wires for the electrical system routed timidly away from interference. The unit can be bolted almost anywhere you wish, but there are a few points of merit to consider first.

Check for clearance all around the depthfinder in your initial choice of location. You don't need the back of the unit jammed against a windshield where the cords will be kinked or rubbed bare with vibration, or where the plug-ins for power and transducer cords must be bent to the side under pressure. Neither do you want the face of the unit perched within inches of the steering wheel where you can't fiddle with the knobs while running. In the case of a graph, lack of clearance in front of the unit will prevent your ability to get in there to change rolls of paper, or make notes, without removing the unit from its mount! Pushed up against the steering wheel, you can't open the door on the face of the graph.

Be certain you have good clearance on all sides of your depthfinder before drilling holes in the console for the mounting bracket. Also check to see what happens when you turn on the unit if you should happen to have a magnetic compass in the same general vicinity. Frequently, the two do not make good neighbors, constantly bickering about priority.

Finally, put your jeans in the driver's seat of the boat and check to see if the unit face is clearly visible from your preferred location for it. Unfortunately, a great many boat consoles are designed with an angle which makes mounting

Surface angles on some boat consoles are not designed to handle simple mounting of depthfinders. This one had to be built up with a 2x8 board.

depthfinders tricky at best. The wood 2x8 bolted on my own console will testify to that fact. I had to raise the mounting surface that much in order to see the face of the dial completely. It also was needed to elevate the power cords so a fella could raise the lid occasionally to get a can of beer from the built-in ice chest located immediately in front of the console!

You might consider the benefits of twisting the bracket slightly toward the passenger side of the boat before making it a permanent fixture. I failed to do this when putting a nifty little graph unit on a boat I had last year, and the results were mixed with regard to results. I did a striper fishing article with lovely Country Music Star Barbara Mandrell. She loves to fish, but had never been exposed to the finer things in life like sonar graphs.

As it was difficult for her to see the images on my graph because it faced straight forward, she was forced (much to my delight) to sit very close to me in order to view the fish and structure as they appeared on the chart. I must admit we caught few fish that afternoon, because I kept riding around the lake while she watched the strange and wonderful things I could do with my depthfinders! However, after she left, I was forced to fish the remainder of the year with far less feminine characters who also practically sat in my lap to see what was going on beneath the boat.

Unless you're in love with your fishing partner, I suggest you turn the depthfinder bracket slightly his way so he can watch the events below, too.

The mechanics of mounting the depthfinder bracket are simple enough. Mark the location for the holes neatly and accurately. Drill the holes and use *large* bolts for securing the bracket to your console. This is quite important to the life of your depthfinder. The vibrations of your boat while pounding waves or a small chop on the water will eventually loosen the bracket if it is not secured heavily. When allowed to rattle and shake, your depthfinder will need a trip to the repairman all too soon. Expensive and sophisticated circuitry was never designed to handle the rigors of life in a paint mixer.

Once the location for your unit has been carefully considered and the mounting bracket securely attached to your boat, you face still another problem. But we're getting near the end of the tunnel now, much to your delight, I'm sure.

The power cord and transducer cord which plug into your unit can be as finicky as a rich bride. Sometimes they will perform admirably in close proximity to other wiring in the boat, and sometimes they seem to pick up the very smallest amount of static from other sources.

Static, or electrical interference, can make your days on the water seem like a week without a Friday. Every time you think you have figured out how to read the signals on your sonar equipment, you will observe miscellaneous images on your flasher or graph which defy interpretation. You must eliminate the problem. And the best time to eliminate the problem from electrical interference is before it happens.

In my opinion, it is keenly important that you wire the depthfinder directly to your main battery instead of plugging the power cord into a spare jack beneath the console. Some sonar manufacturers agree with me; some don't. Going straight to the main battery avoids possible noise pick-up from other equipment in the boat. The experts all agree on that. At least one sonar expert, Pat McCann in Houston, Texas, says if you wire the depthfinder through the dashboard it *can* make a change in the negative lead which goes to that dashboard. This can cause electrolysis in the transducer, and, in time, will eat up the transducer completely.

Other problems which could come from a dashboard hook-up include a slight loss of power in the connection, or in the size wire used by the boat builder, and a power loss resulting from running various accessories in the boat simultaneously with the depthfinder. Why gamble? Most depthfinders come equipped with sufficient lengths of power cord to reach from mid-ships to the battery compartment. Spend

*Be sure to fuse the unit in your boat; overheated wires
can cause a fire hazard.*

another 79 cents for tape to hold the wire out of your way as
it runs from the unit to the battery.

You face the challenge of trying to calculate how to
route the depthfinder power cord and the wire from the
transducer so that neither of them get chummy with other
electrical wires in your boat. This can be a trifle frustrating,
especially when the wiring for so many modern bass boats
looks like an octopus hatchery. Organize that mess to the
best of your ability, and tape the wires for your depthfinder
out of the way. Creativity has its certain rewards. The little
plastic ties you can buy at Ace Hardware are great for this.

Run the transducer cord along a path which will keep it
the maximum distance away from all other wires in the
boat, especially those in the electrical system of your big
engine and its tachometer. Flexible metal conduit, plastic

hose pipe and liberal layers of electrical tape wrapped around the cord will all help shield the transducer cord from unwanted interference.

I recommend you install a small fuse breaker on the positive wire going from the depthfinder to your battery. You can purchase these nifty little pieces of insurance from practically any automotive parts dealer, splice them into the wire, and rest easy on the water while the sonar unit is in operation. The Owner's Manual which comes with your depthfinder should reveal detail on the appropriate size fuse to use, but if it omits this data, try a four-amp fuse for safety. Overheated wires can cause a fire hazard, and fuses are quite cheap when compared to replacing a whole boat! The fuse should be inserted into the positive lead approximately 12 inches from the battery.

There is far more to installing a depthfinder system in your boat than most people would think. If the installation of your transducer or the unit wiring is done poorly, you will have lost a great deal of efficiency before ever going to the water.

Aluminum Hulls: Unanswered Controversy

In the four or more years following my research for the original edition of this book, advances in sonar technology have been fantastic. However, there was one question raised back then which still has not been totally answered. Almost. But not 100% proven. The question is: Can you shoot a signal from your transducer through an aluminum boat hull effectively?

Sides were clearly drawn on the issue back in 1981–82. Brand X manufacturer stated a very positive "yes," while Brand Y said "no" with equal conviction. Nobody had done enough controlled testing to make a positive statement of fact. Given the growing popularity of aluminum fishing boats at the time, "through the hull" abilities of transducers in aluminum boats was an important consideration. Obviously, it still is today.

Aluminum boats have special characteristics which definitely affect the performance of your depthfinder transducer, whether mounted inside or on the transom.

When considering inside, or through-the-hull mounting, consider that different manufacturers construct their hulls in a variety of thicknesses. Some are coated with a layer or two of paint, while others are "raw" metal. Then too, there are differences in alloy content between aluminum types. Construction techniques make some aluminum boats quite rigid, others rather flexible. This means some tin boats vibrate a lot while running; some do not. All of these factors affect the efficiency with which your transducer can perform.

Whether mounting your transducer inside the boat or hanging off the transom, remember that aluminum boats are literally "built" a piece at a time, not poured or sprayed into a mold for single-piece construction. Pieces of metal are cut, then assembled together with rivets and/or welds. Those welded spots and rivet heads, plus any keels, steps, runners or scoops for the livewell plug, all create water turbulence as the boat runs across the lake. That turbulence takes the form of air bubbles which flow under the hull and exit beneath the transom. As you remember from earlier comments, transducers cannot shoot a signal effectively through air. Or air bubbles.

Aluminum boats are literally built one piece at a time.
The resulting welds and rivet heads can create water
turbulence forward of your transducer,
causing problems.

Life is further complicated for the tin boat sonar user if
you think about the typical manner in which these rigs
bounce their flat little bottoms over the waterways. Even on
very smooth water, the moment your engine raises your flat-
bottom fishing machine onto plane, you begin to trap air
under the hull. The bow goes up, air hits the flat undersur-
face, and the air gets trapped momentarily while it passes
under the hull. A light chop on the water produces an
excessive amount of air traveling beneath the hull.

Weight distribution in the boat can be used to combat
the problems. The more batteries, gas cans and concrete
blocks you stack in the general vicinity of the transducer,
the further down in the water that particular portion of the

boat will ride. The more weight you place forward, the lower the bow will ride when on plane.

Mounting your transducer on the transom, and dropping it down well below the level of your hull, is one answer. One large manufacturer markets a bracket today designed to do exactly that. Presumably, running thru the water an inch or two beneath the hull, your transducer couldn't care less about all the fuss just above its head.

Citing personal experience with an aluminum rig I used for several years, I was unable to get good readings when I tried to shoot signals through the hull. This does not mean another tin rig with different gauge metal, alloy content, etc., would not have worked fine. In my case, it seemed the *entire hull* became something of a sounding board for the transducer pulses, and the returning info was pretty fuzzy.

I hung the transducer off the transom, building a bridge of silicone to smooth the gap. The location was selected in the manner previously described for finding "smooth water" exiting beneath the transom. As I personally care absolutely nothing about running 75 mph in a flat-bottom aluminum boat, the installation worked admirably for my fishing needs. When searching for structure, cranking up the sensitivity on my unit made it possible to see changes in bottom contour and/or treetops easily while motoring along at moderate speeds. "Moderate" speed to me means my hair doesn't tickle my ears while underway.

By all means, experiment with the mounting method in your aluminum boat. It is quite possible you will be able to find a spot inside the boat where you can shoot a signal effectively from your transducer. It is equally possible you will lose far too much detail to employ through-the-hull mounting. Compare signals shot through the metal with

signals generated from hand-holding the transducer over the side. You be the judge. I think you'll probably opt for a transom mount when it's all over.

All who use aluminum boats in the process of filling freezers with fillets should be aware of the inherent problems to be encountered when either shooting a transducer signal through the hull or merely hanging one over the transom. There is nothing wrong with your choice of boats, but you must adapt your sonar mounting procedure to overcome the obstacles.

It's a little like a single man trying to decide if he wants to spend his time and money with an attractive divorcee, an eager-to-please-and-learn 19 year-old, or a married woman only interested in certain parts of his anatomy. Each choice has advantages and drawbacks.

One major depthfinder manufacturer suggests the following procedure for mounting a transducer to shoot signals through the hull:

Figure 1
Select a clean, flat surface area between the
grooves or rivets (aluminum boats) in the hull,
and sand the area smoothly to insure
good contact.

Figure 2
Mix two-part epoxy cement thoroughly for sev-
eral minutes, then apply a liberal amount of the
cement onto the face of the transducer.
Spread evenly.

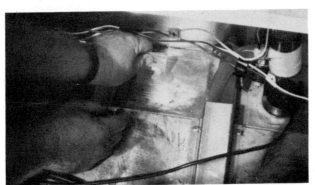

Figure 3
*Any remaining epoxy is applied to the inside hull
location for the transducer.*

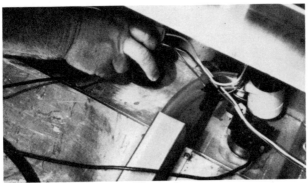

Figure 4
*Position the transducer in the selected location
and use a circular motion to squeeze out
all air bubbles.*

Figure 5
Press down firmly and hold the transducer in place for a few minutes to complete the job.

Figure 6
Properly affixed, the transducer should perform at all speeds.

A Second Depthfinder Up Front

Having two depthfinders in the boat definitely makes life easier for the fisherman. You can cruise the lake searching for a likely spot with a console-mounted unit, traveling at whatever speed you choose. Once fish are found, the big engine is killed, and so is the console depthfinder. The bow-mounted second unit then takes the spotlight on stage as it allows you to center the boat over your quarry and hold it there with a little help from the trolling motor.

Placement of the front transducer is optional. A few fiberglass boats are designed with front cut-outs in the hull for mounting the forward transducer. This will work fine when the boat is resting, but not while running on plane. When the boat is up and going, the bow normally is lifted out of the water by the steps, lifters and strakes built into the hull, and this would, of course, put air between the hull and the water up front.

Another choice of location for the second transducer would be back on the transom again. This is not a particularly good place for it, as the signals you would be reading from the bow-mounted unit would be some 10 or 15 feet away from your tennis shoes instead of directly below them. Fish you see on your depthfinder would be fish living beneath your transom, not under the bow. Vertical jigging for fish 15 feet away from your lure is not often very productive.

The ideal place for mounting your front unit transducer is on the foot of your trolling motor. You can't run the big engine on the boat while the trolling motor is in the water, but it really doesn't matter because the initial unit on the console will be used while cruising anyway. With the pod mounted on the trolling motor, fish you see will be fish right under your feet.

Credit: Tennessee Wildlife Resources Agency

When boats increase speed and get up on plane, the
bow normally rises out of the water. Transducers used
for reading at cruising speeds must be mounted
in rear third of boat.

There are three easy procedures for mounting a transducer on your trolling motor. The most simple is to take a
glob of silicone, apply it to the *top* of the puck, and squash it
onto the bottom of the motor housing. String or rubber
bands will hold the puck in place while the silicone dries.
Route the cord well clear of the prop and on up the shaft,
using plastic ties. Silicone is fine for this as there should be
no oil spills there.

Some manufacturers supply an oversize radiator hose
clamp, and build "ears" on their transducer for use in
mounting on the trolling motor. Insert the clamp through the
holes in the ears, take it on around the motor housing and
then tighten the screw to hold everything in place. Simple
and efficient. Route the cord in the same manner as above.

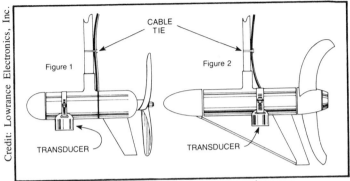

Credit: Lowrance Electronics, Inc.

Typical Trolling Motor Mounting

There is a third method for mounting the puck on the electric motor which is rather unconventional, but works quite well. It also can solve problems in mounting when the top surface of the transducer is not designed to fit against the bottom of the housing. See if you can find one of the rubber suction cups that comes with a transducer designed for sticking onto the boat without permanent mounting. Other type suction cups will work, provided they are large enough and can be attached to a bracket.

The suction cup is mated with a transducer bracket, and the puck installed in the bracket. The suction cup is then pushed against the bottom of the motor housing, and held there securely with a pair of plastic ties. In this manner, you can mount a transducer which was never designed to fit flush with the bottom of your trolling motor, and it will perform admirably. In addition, the short stem on the rubber cup will flex slightly, cushioning any contact with stumps and rocks in shallow water.

Bow-mounted depthfinders are usually placed in the boat a bit forward of the front seat where they can be read easily while fishing from that location. I again recommend

With a little ingenuity you can install a transducer on the trolling motor even if the puck was not designed to fit there. The mount starts with a suction cup and appropriate bracket.

you wire the unit directly to the main battery in your boat. Should the power cord for your depthfinder not quite reach the distance from bow to battery, you can extend it the needed inches (or feet) with automotive primary wire, #12 or #14. If you wish to solder the connection between the two wires, use a rosin-core solder, not one with an acid core.

Concluding Comments

Before closing out this chapter on transducers, I might mention that with a few boats the most simple method for installing your transducer is not to install it at all! If your boat has an enclosed sump area, and *the hull directly beneath it is of single-layer construction,* this may work for you.

All you have to do is pour about an inch of water into the sump, place your transducer in with it, and go fishing. The water retained in the sump will keep the face of the puck well-wetted, and it shoots signals right through the hull perfectly. You don't have to cement the puck to the floor, just toss it in there and be sure the water is deep enough to cover it.

There are a couple of problems with this procedure. You must keep the sump area clean and free of oil or gas spills. You could drop a bar of Ivory soap into the water with the transducer, and this will aid in preventing oil from coating the eye. It would be wise to clean out the sump area often also, for the same reason. And if you hit rough water, making the transducer bounce around a bit, you may have to reach back there afterwards and stand it upright again. Still, this is certainly the easiest way to ''mount'' a transducer if your boat design will allow it.

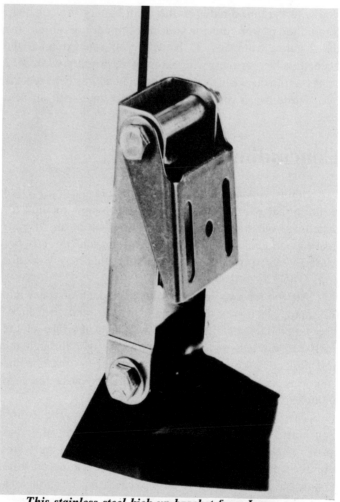

This stainless steel kick-up bracket from Lowrance may be the answer to owners of aluminum boats who want effective readings from their transducers. It positions the "eye" of your unit beneath the turbulence created by typical aluminum hulls.

It will be mentioned again in this book, but I must emphasize that the eye of your transducer can become totally blinded if allowed to contact oil for any material period of time. Oil apparently soaks into the face of the transducer, first reducing its sensitivity a good deal, then finally coating the surface sufficiently to ruin its operation totally. Transom-mounted transducers are subject to contact with oil just sitting in a busy marina. Road film accumulated in transit to and from the lake can build up on a transducer, also. It is keenly important that you keep the face of your transducer clean. Wash it often with warm water and soap. Obviously, this does not apply to transducers cemented into the hull inside the boat, but you should check on them occasionally, too. Be sure no cracks in the cement have developed which would allow oil or gas to seep under the pod.

3

Operating Procedures

Basic Operations

Properly installed and functioning, a depthfinder will produce a wealth of valuable information for fishermen. The amount of information you get is limited only by the circuitry purchased and your personal ability to read and interpret the signals.

It is a simple fact of life that expertise in reading your sonar unit does not come quickly. It doesn't even come slowly. It comes *very* slowly. Some of the advertisements for sonar units make it all sound quite easy, but out there in the lake where fish are to be found, it just doesn't work that way. Learning to understand all the information your depthfinder is providing requires a great many hours of serious work, study and experimenting. Most of which should take place on the water.

In this chapter we are going to take an in-depth look at how to operate your sonar equipment correctly. You should find plenty of information here that was not spelled out in the instruction manual which came with your unit. Hope-

The most common mistake made with depthfinder use is failure to turn the sensitivity control up sufficiently.

fully, the following will save you a tremendous number of hours trying to figure it all out by trial and error.

The things you are about to read are all based upon having properly installed your transducer and having made correct electrical connections for the unit.

The Controls

Sensitivity Control. My friend Randy Fite, an expert on depthfinders in his own right, once told me the most common mistake people make with their depthfinder takes place when they turn the switch on! And it's true. His observation is backed by several other experts on sonar, and even hinted at in a few Owner's Manuals put out by manufacturers.

The "Off/On" switch for a depthfinder is the power control, acting pretty much like the volume knob on a radio. It also performs the job of "fine tuning" the frequency just as the other knob on a radio is used to zero in on a station for the best reception. The Gain, or Sensitivity Control as it is often called, simply activates the unit and then increases the power to the receiver in the unit in relation to how far the knob is rotated. The more you "turn the volume up," the more power you have, and the more sensitivity you get.

Randy says most people turn on their depthfinder, continue rotating the sensitivity knob until they get a bottom reading, and then stop right there. "Stopping right there" is the mistake.

If you continue to turn up the power, you will get a second reading, or "echo," at exactly twice the actual bottom depth. This is caused by part of the initial signal coming back to the top of the lake after striking the bottom, bouncing off the water surface itself (and/or the hull of your boat) and being reflected back down to the bottom where it strikes *again* and is bounced upwards for the second time. Due to the time elapsed while making two trips down and back, the second echo will be picked up on your unit, appearing at twice the actual depth of the bottom. Were it not for the fact high-frequency sonar signals are partially absorbed by the objects they strike, the routine might go on forever.

Credit: Tennessee Wildlife Resources Agency

When you pass over a very hard bottom (like an old road bed, for example) you immediately can see an increase in multiple bottom readings, each appearing on the unit in increments of the actual depth. *Hard surfaces reflect more of the signal than soft surfaces,* a keenly important fact to remember later in this book.

Anyhow, having more than one bottom reading on the depthfinder annoys many people, so they turn down the sensitivity until only one can be seen. The trouble is, reducing the unit's power like that may rob it of the needed sensitivity to pick up and display the smaller, weaker underwater echoes. You know, like the ones that come from fish. . .

There are other valuable benefits in having a second bottom reading shown on your depthfinder in addition to furnishing sufficient power for displaying weaker signals. These will be explained momentarily. But for now, remember that giving your depthfinder enough power and sensitivity to create a second bottom echo will also give it enough muscle to display fish.

As you increase the power to your unit the initial bottom reading will become wider on both flashers and graphs. This in no way affects what the unit is telling you about the correct water depth. The band, or bottom signal, will widen in a *downward* direction only. The top of that reading remains constant, showing the accurate distance between your transducer and the bottom of the lake. The reason the bottom reading expands is because part of your signal is being absorbed by the bottom itself, thus delaying the return echo slightly. That moving wheel or belt on your unit turns too fast to be seen by the human eye, so it's only reasonable that even a fractional difference in the time lapse for a returning signal would be shown further down the scale.

There are times when a second bottom echo is not desirable. When you are fishing with a flasher unit and the bottom depth exceeds half the maximum depth on the face of your unit, the second reading would appear somewhere in the area on the dial where you hope to see fish signals. Example: on a flasher with a 60-foot depth scale, a second echo for the bottom in 40-foot water would show up at 20 feet on the face of the unit. $(40+40-60=20)$. This may be the exact depth you hope to find huge stripers waiting for your offering, and it would be tough to separate their signals from those created by the second bottom echo. In this case, turn the sensitivity control down only until the second reading fades. The stripers will generate bright signals at 20 feet, not weak ones.

Depth Scales. Many sonar units have two or more depth scales from which to choose. A flip of the switch or a pull on the knob will convert the overall depth scale from one set of numbers to another. Advantages here are numerous. As mentioned, when water depth exceeds half the maximum reading on your flasher, the second echo from the bottom can interfere with your ability to read fish signals in the productive zone. If you have the multiple-scale feature on your unit, you can switch over to a deeper scale and eliminate the problem. On graph units, when the water depth exceeds the *total* depth shown on a particular scale, the bottom reading simply disappears completely. In this case, you switch to a deeper scale to find the bottom again.

It is important that you adjust the sensitivity control to handle the deeper scale settings. Usually, changing over to a deeper depth scale on a sonar unit requires an increase in power to maintain maximum readout efficiency.

Under some conditions, it can be very advantageous to switch to a very shallow depth scale on graphs. This allows

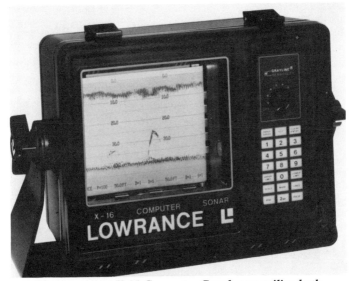

*The Lowrance X-16 Computer Graph can utilize both
192 and 50 kHz transducers, interfaces with Loran-C,
has automatic suppression system.*

the unit to display detail over the entire width of the paper.
The enlarged detail makes it much easier to identify fish and
structure type. In the case of suspended fish, you could even
sacrifice getting a bottom reading at all!

Most graphs and video units today are programmed to
allow the selection of a specific band or layer of water
below, and then expand the detail full-size on the paper or
screen. You merely enter the upper and lower limits in
desired depth, and the machine does the rest. Your choice
may be flexible, as with a moving cursor on video, or
broken into predetermined increments.

As a general rule, I suggest you use the most shallow
depth scale on both flashers and graphs which allows the

unit to cover the total water depth. This makes it much easier to read the signals, and is far less confusing. However, when the bottom drops materially, switch over to a deeper depth scale and crank up the sensitivity a bit.

Suppressor Knob. This particular adjustment on your sonar helper should be eyed with caution like a shabbily-dressed bill collector. The suppressor is designed to filter out unwanted interference in your unit, much like the squelch control in a CB radio. Sometimes, like over-eager salesmen, it doesn't know when to stop performing. Although use of the suppressor control generally does not affect the unit's sensitivity, it has an adverse effect on the way some of the smaller underwater objects are displayed.

The suppressor causes a "blending" phenomenon. Small objects close together in the water frequently are displayed on the face of your equipment as a single image. Fish relaxing close to the bottom can be merged into the bottom signals and never be seen. Three or four small fish getting friendly in a small area could be shown as a single trophy worthy of attention, etc.

Unwanted noise from your electrical system, or the engine's ignition, can create false signals to appear on your depthfinder. Air bubbles on the transducer can do the same thing. Cavitation in the prop while running can screw up readings, also. These "noise" problems are why your unit has a suppressor control. *Slight* use of the suppressor will normally make them go away. Just remember that the less suppression control used, the better will be the resolution between individual objects below. At slow boat speeds, no suppression should be needed.

While we are talking about the use of the suppressor control on your depthfinder, it seems only appropriate to talk about the cause and elimination of unwanted signal

Kentucky Department of Fish & Wildlife Resources

"static" which could appear on your depthfinder. The suppressor circuitry should be used only as a "last ditch" effort to clarify readings. Problems causing static interference usually can be eliminated before use of this feature is needed. If you experience numerous unwanted static signals on your depthfinder, even while running at slow speeds, try the following procedure to eliminate the source(s):

- Turn off the big engine and allow the boat to come to a complete stop in the water. All static signals should then disappear. If not, check to see if there is any other electrical equipment running in the boat. If the problem is coming from some accessory you are running, you must rewire the gadget if you wish to use it simultaneously with the depthfinder.

- If all static interference disappears when the boat stops moving and the engine is killed, your problem was caused by either engine ignition interference or by air bubbles on the transducer. To find out which is the culprit, put the engine in neutral and rev it up pretty good. If the static comes back, you know the engine's electrical system is at fault. You will be required to re-route the wires going to your depthfinder, keeping them further away from all electrical wires to the big engine. You may be forced to encase the transducer cord in a plastic hose, wrap it several times with electrical tape, or maybe choose a different type spark plug for your engine. Contact the engine manufacturer for suggestions about how to reduce ignition interference.

• If the above remedy fails, you are getting excess air turbulence on the face of your transom-mounted transducer, or you are getting cavitation noises from the prop. Adjust the transducer angle of attack. Check to see if any silicone bridge between hull and transducer has broken or wrinkled. Slide the puck further down into the water on its bracket. If that doesn't succeed, find another location for mounting your transducer, preferably locating it a bit further away from the prop.

Other Important Features. Most graphs have an additional pair of controls not found on flashers. Both are rather dramatic in the results they can produce. The *chart speed* control determines the speed at which paper is fed through the graph. The *grayline* or *whiteline* control shades the bottom reading for easier identification of objects near the bottom.

Most of us are cautious with the money we spend, and

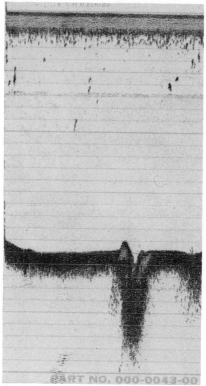

Small ditch on bottom appears compressed without
detail due to very slow paper speed.

therefore tend to be stingy on the subject of chart speed. At
an average of six bucks per roll of graph paper, we often fail
to see the advantage of running the stuff through our graph
at maximum speed. Yet there are many times when a fast
chart speed is quite necessary for getting meaningful
readout on the paper.

The most easily-understood example will occur when

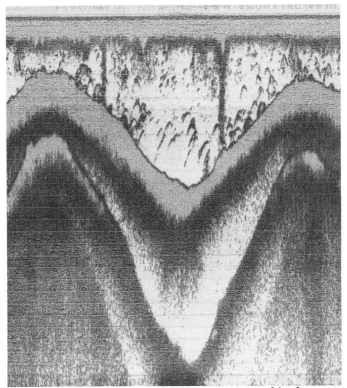

Faster paper speed used while crossing over this channel allows graph to draw in details of fish and structure.

you motor across a small creek bed looking for fish and productive structure. With the paper speed set at a slow pace, details of the creek bed, and everything in it, will appear compressed tightly together. You may see little more than a ''crack'' in the bottom. This is because you passed over the creek bed and exited across the far shoulder before the graph paper had time to draw out the details for you.

*Impulse's Micro Trac 6100 Video is a 200 kHz unit
with four depth ranges.*

Conversely, the use of a higher paper speed would have allowed the graph to expand, or spread out, the detail as you went over the area. Instead of seeing only a thin crack in the earth below, you would be able to observe the drop-off on both sides of the creek, structure in the channel and probably fish relaxing nearby. So here you see the advantage in using a fast paper speed on your graph: you get more detail and you see it more clearly, at least most of the time. In principle, the same goes for video sweep speed.

When talking about chart paper speed for getting better detail, the discussion must include a few phrases on the subject of boat speed, also. As a general rule, the faster the boat is moving, the faster the chart speed necessary to keep up. It follows that the slower the boat moves, the slower you can run the paper through the machine without suffering a

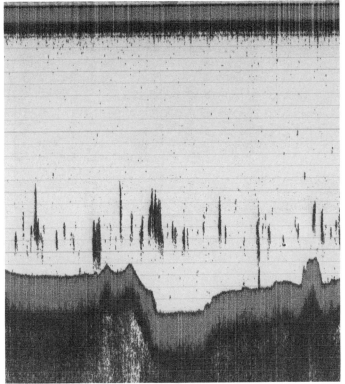

*Excessively slow paper speed while cruising can force
fish images to be drawn as near-straight, vertical lines
instead of typical arches.*

great loss of detail. Beyond those generalities, you will be
forced to experiment with your own set-up, trying different
combos of boat/paper speeds until you find out the system
which compresses the least detail for you on carbon-backed
pine trees or micro chip imagery.

Very slow paper speed will distort the typical arched

figure drawn by the graph as you pass over fish, causing them to appear as near-straight vertical lines. Excessively slow boat speed will stretch out fish signals because the critter remains beneath the transducer for longer periods of time. In this case, instead of getting the arched image on the graph, you observe a long, almost straight horizontal line. An extreme example of this would be where the boat, transducer and fish were all sitting still. Only the graph paper is moving. You would see the bottom reading and a straight line representing the depth of the fish which just kept on, and on, and on.

You will have to run many rolls of graph paper through

your machine before mastering the proper relation between boat speed and chart paper speed under a variety of conditions.

The grayline or whiteline control on many graphs also can be a bit on the tricky side to use effectively. Its function is to shade away the heavy black mass drawn on the paper immediately below where the bottom reading is shown, leaving in its place a single black line representing the correct bottom depth. This exercise in electronic genius makes it far easier to distinguish trees and brush on the bottom, and makes it even easier to spot fish holding near the bottom.

Still another advantage of the grayline feature comes in

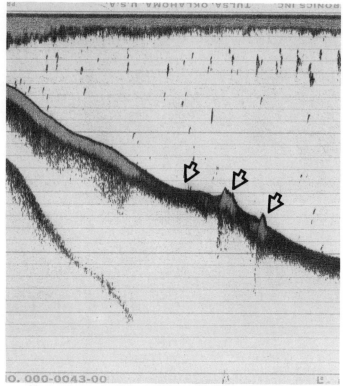

Notice how width of whiteline (shaded bottom) is wide when passing over hard surface, narrows and disappears when over soft bottom. Also note two rock piles picked out on bottom and displayed easily on graph because of this feature.

determining the bottom composition. Hard bottoms will cause the gray area to get wider on the graph. When the bottom changes to mud or vegetation, the signals are weaker and the gray area shrinks automatically.

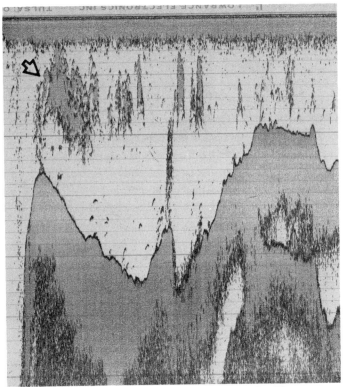

Excessive use of whiteline/grayline control will cause shading of mid-range objects, making interpretation harder. Note fish signals here which have been shaded in this manner.

Excess use of the grayline control will cause unwanted shading of all large objects in the water. Big fish, schools of smaller fish, treetops and other things in the water will be shaded just like the bottom, making it harder to figure out accurately what you are seeing on the paper.

Miscellaneous Points About Operation

Very high boat speed will compress the detail on your graph, regardless of the paper speed. High boat speed will make the "blips" on a flasher almost impossible to read, too. You can observe bottom depth fairly accurately on a depthfinder while the boat is steaming along (providing you have a darn good transducer installation), but reading detail accurately on either a flasher or graph when the boat is traveling in excess of 30 mph will be virtually impossible.

With some graphs, turning the sensitivity control wide open will cause excessive black printing (or burning, to be more correct) on the paper. The detail will have a tendency to smear, and the carbon build-up gets pretty bad. These units are designed to be turned up until you get a good second bottom reading only. Their ability to provide power beyond this point is reserved for deeper water situations. The smearing effect makes it tough to read the images accurately, and the excess dust created while burning the paper makes it necessary to clean away the particles inside the case frequently.

Do not increase the white/grayline control knob sufficiently to shade the *second* bottom echo. Only the first bottom reading should be shaded. This has nothing to do with the amount of sensitivity you give to the unit.

Engineers at SI-TEX (Smith's Industries, Inc.) suggest that 1,200 to 1,400 rpm with an 85 hp engine on a 16-foot boat will produce optimum boat speed for charting detail on their graphs. They also recommend the paper speed on their graphs be set at maximum rate at all times.

Increasing sensitivity on any depthfinder, flasher or

graph will improve the unit's ability to display fish signals from the outer edge of the transducer cone.

Slower paper speeds generate slightly darker images on graph paper.

Excess sensitivity control usage results in very dark images drawn on the graph paper, sometimes making them hard to read and interpret. Concentrations of plankton and bait fish in the water are likely to be shown as a single huge mass, giving rise to fears that Jaws III is prowling around in your lake.

In the original edition of this book I made the statement that you cannot operate two depthfinders of similar frequency in your boat at the same time. This is because the units will pick up signals from each other, causing a "cartwheel" effect on flashers, and pure jumble on a graph (see next illustration). There are machines on the market today which solve the problem by using a filtering pro-

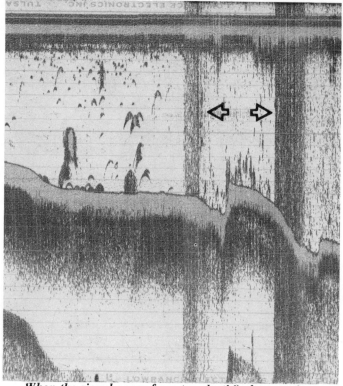

When the signal cones from two depthfinders overlap,
they fight. Here you see the results from turning on a
second unit in the boat while the graph
was still running.

cedure which separates the signals. However, unless *both* units in your boat have this feature, one of them is going to be affected anyway. The same holds true for depthfinders operating in other boats nearby. Most depthfinders in use today are still prima donnas.

The fish you see on your depthfinder probably are not

Credit: Vexilar, Inc.

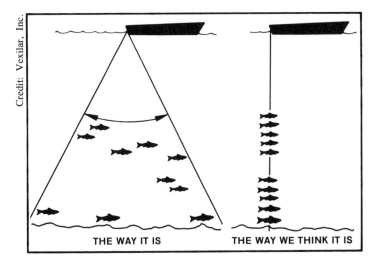

THE WAY IT IS   THE WAY WE THINK IT IS

as close together as they appear. This is due to the mechanical transition which occurs by taking everything within a circle of viewing area and placing it onto a flat plane. The transducer cone of signals covers several feet of real estate on the bottom, and the fish you see displayed can be anywhere within that area. They are not stacked on top of each other down there.

The deeper in the water fish signals appear, the more likely it is that the fish itself is off to one side or the other from your boat. This is due to the spread of the cone as it goes down, and the Law of Averages which says only a small part of the fish in a given circle will be directly under your transducer at any particular time. In the case of a graph unit, you can see when the fish is closest to your transducer by observing when the peak of the arch appears. But this still doesn't mean his tail is directly beneath your transducer.

A narrowing of the whiteline on a graph will indicate

Credit: Techsonic Industries, Inc.

Humminbird's Mark V Flasher features a 100-foot depth scale.

you are passing over a soft spot in the bottom as mentioned previously. On flasher units (or graphs not sporting the whiteline feature), you can discover changes in the bottom composition by observing the *second echo* reading. Remember how important we told you that second reading was? Passing over soft bottom will make the second echo fade away or disappear completely. Hard bottom, rocks and gravel, or an old roadbed will generate sharp, bright multiple bottom echoes. Soft bottom absorbs; hard bottom reflects. That's a tidy bit of info when you're searching for the

best location to string your trot-line, ambush a sauger or entice a hungry smallmouth.

You may not have a memory like a filing cabinet, and all this information may take a while to soak in fully. But even more important, you might need a little help initially building confidence in your depthfinder. Just because the thing says bottom is 36 feet under your hull, how do you know it ain't lying? Take a measured line and test it. Neither people nor machines are always perfect. People do seem to exhibit weakness more often than machines, but it is possible your depthfinder has a couple of cross-eyed circuits, or maybe a whatszit that makes the wheels spin out of sync.

*Accurate notes made on his graph paper last winter
allowed this angler to return to the same spot this year
and duplicate the fun.*

Use a measured line to prove your unit is telling the truth about the bottom depth. If that checks out O.K., you can trust the rest of the information. Confidence in your depth-finder makes it much easier to use effectively. It won't lie to you.

The "marker button" on some graph units can be used as an aid in reconstructing water situations and locations later when you are at home reviewing the day's progress on the chart paper. All the button does for you is draw a solid black line down the width of the paper. But you can use one line to indicate Point A, two lines to indicate Point B, etc. Work out your own code system, and use a pencil to record other important info on the chart paper for future reference. In this manner, you can build a fine fishing library of the action you encounter on the lake day after day. It doesn't matter whether you fish tournaments or try to fill the family freezer, that record can be valuable the next year when you return to the same spot at the same time of year. With a little luck from the weatherman and Mother Nature, fish will be in the same place at the same time, year after year. And they probably will hit the same lures if you care to record that, also.

Operating a depthfinder properly comes with practice and time spent on the water. I have used the word ''experiment'' more than a few times in the preceding pages. With serious practice, and serious hours spent on the water reading your sonar equipment signals, you can learn to understand the information your unit provides. It will be your own desire to learn and the amount of time you devote to the learning process that determines how far you can go with sonar.

I caution you not to become discouraged easily. Sonar readings are like women in high-class barrooms. It usually takes more than one drink to figure out what they are really saying to you. And you might even compare barroom society with depthfinder efficiency by saying you can spend a lot of money on both and still not get what you want if your method of operation is poor.

Next, we examine various ways to interpret the signals, and apply what your depthfinder tells you to the weight of your stringer.

4
Signal Interpretation

What the Heck Is *That*?

Interpreting sonar signals is tough. Especially so, because everything keeps changing around in the water. Temperature, clarity, algae levels, fish movements, even the season of the year will alter what you see displayed on your sonar flasher or graph. Regardless of the time of year, the species of fish you seek, etc., one thing will remain constant. You will, without fail, see *something* on the face of your unit which you don't completely understand!

Among experts and beginners alike, the most often asked question while watching the running depthfinder is, "What the heck is *that*?"

This particular chapter on depthfinders is by far the most difficult to put down on paper. It deals with how to interpret the signals you see on your sonar equipment. Before getting into the nuts and bolts of sonar interpretation, I feel obligated to make two statements:

      1—There is absolutely no substitute for personal experience in building your expertise for interpreting sonar signals.

2—*Nobody* can interpret accurately every single mark or flash on a depthfinder.

It is only fair to tell you these chapters "build" one upon the other. Comments below are predicated upon your having installed your transducer correctly, and upon your having learned how to operate the controls on your depthfinder with some degree of efficiency. These comments on how to interpret signals will not prove accurate if you have failed in either of the above requirements.

Starting Fresh with Sonar

The first time you leave the dock with a spanking new depthfinder installed in your boat, be ready for a surprise when you turn on the switch. You likely will begin seeing all sorts of things beneath the surface almost immediately, even before you pass the "No Wake" buoys.

Nope. At that speed there is nothing wrong with your unit. You can bet your gas money that the objects your sonar machine displays on its face are really down there. Hundreds of them.

The trick is to figure out what all those images represent. Some of them are baitfish. Others are game fish. The "Christmas tree" light-up is probably just that: an underwater treetop. That single image displayed momentarily was probably a lonesome bass or a misguided crappie away from its friends.

A topographical map of the lake will prove most helpful when you begin "fishing" with 12 volts. The pros use these things to find structure whenever possible, and you can do the same with your map. At this point, forget about fishing for the moment and concentrate on finding various types of underwater structure to look over. Drive the boat to

*Use of a topographical map will greatly ease the initial
learning process for signal interpretation.*

a sloping point which goes out into the lake from the
shoreline. Drive back and forth across it, watching how the
depthfinder signals come up gradually from the bottom,
bounce around a bit while you're over the top of the point,
and then taper back down slowly as you exit the far side.
Observe how the bottom signals widen slightly as you go
over the edge of the point. This is because your signal cone
is recording bottom at more than one depth along the slope
simultaneously. That bouncing around business while

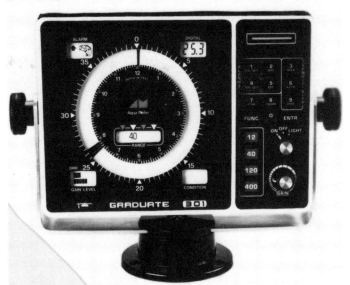

The Graduate from Aqua Meter has eight ranges, zoom, a digital readout, filters out false echoes.

you're on top of the point (or slightly off to one side) is probably due to some stumps or brush there.

Continue using the map to find underwater trees, stump rows, old river channels, sharp drop-offs, etc. Each will produce a distinct type signal on your depthfinder. You may not be able to recognize it at first, but keep running the boat over these things and let the signals soak into your memory banks. Put away the map and run to another part of the lake. Check the signals you see and try to identify the type underwater structure below. Then take a peek at the map to see if you were correct. When you can identify various types of bottom structure pretty well, you are ready for the next step.

The thing I have noticed most about fishing with other people who have depthfinders in their boats is that they frequently cannot put their boat over the same spot twice in a row. We motor along searching for fish until something promising pops up on the depthfinder. Then the guy says, "Hey! There they are!" and cuts the throttle back. He eases the boat around, goes back to where he thinks the fish are, and the depthfinder shows a blank. Granted, sometimes the boat will spook fish when it passes over them. But most of the time, the boat driver simply cannot return to the same spot after he once passes over it. Wind, current or a pure lack of any real sense of direction will usually complicate the routine. It isn't all that easy to go back to the exact spot on the water where you saw fish signals.

Practice. Practice. Practice.

Find a reasonably large piece of structure on the bottom which juts upward. A single big stump, a solitary treetop, large boulder, etc. Anything unusual which stands out on the bottom will do for this exercise.

Find the large stump, or whatever, and drive the boat over it. Then practice turning slowly so as not to spook the stump, and drive your boat right back to it, stopping when the stump is directly beneath your boat. You will find this critically-important ability to be much more difficult than you might imagine. You will also need a rather generous frustration quotient before mastering the technique. It's like the fella says about hitting the center of a 100-yard rifle target, "There's a lot of space all *around* the bull's-eye!" There's a lot of water all around that stump, too. And if you're a few feet off to one side or the other when you come back by, you'll never see it.

A lot of fishermen use floating marker buoys to simplify the task. This is fine, but I have decided the aver-

age fish doesn't care much for having a heavy lead weight dropped on his head just so you can come back to the spot again. This is especially true of bass and stripers, who routinely swim away from large falling weights. In this case, you can return to the exact spot again, but the fish won't be there.

You may find it handy to develop the habit of noting a few landmarks when you pass over fish. By making mental notes like: "the big red oak was lined up with the little green drink can on the bank," you can ease the problem of putting your boat back where you want it. Out in open water where landmarks are more elusive, you can drop over a floating buoy several feet *beyond* where the fish are spotted. Then return to the marker, go past it the appropriate distance, and

look for your fillets. It helps to remember which side of the school you dropped the marker on.

As you begin to get a clear idea of how various bottom structures appear on your depthfinder, you will be ready to start work on the goodies which appear somewhere between the top and bottom of the lake. Mid-depth readings are usually "where the action is" on sonar. A lake of average fertility will produce literally thousands of mid-depth readings for you to enjoy.

Reading Fish Signals

Now we're getting into the good stuff. We can go fishing at last.

If you have a fair understanding of fish habitat, you should have an easier time in this phase of your education. Years ago, some people thought largemouth bass were invented by the Corps of Engineers. Today, we know this is not true. Stumps, logs and drop-offs invented them. As a bonus, they invented bream, catfish, crappie and muskies, too. With this firmly in your mind, you must understand that different types of fish can relate to different types of structure, water temperature, depth and so forth. Then when the winter comes, they pack their pebbles and vacation in somebody else's home.

This business of finding fish in relation to structure (habitat) is pretty much a proven fact, with the possible exception of carp. And I have a suspicion that people with an affinity for carp fishing would probably prefer to spend their money on doughballs than depthfinders. I could be wrong. To continue, you might spot a big fish sitting alone out in the middle of the lake well away from any structure. If so, you might wager it's a carp because no self-respecting bass would consider commuting.

If you plan to use sonar signals to find game fish living around structure in the lake, it follows you should be able to tell the difference between trees and fish scales, right? Otherwise, you'll end up fishing in a ''school'' of tree branches, much to the disgust of your depthfinder. In order to learn how to see fish, and tell them apart from structure, I suggest you purchase a few dozen small jigs.

Pick jigs or grubs in a style and size popular on your particular lake; ones known to take a variety of species:

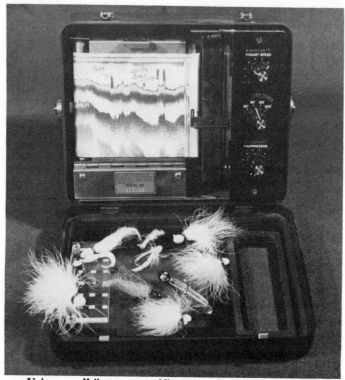

Using small jigs to prove/disprove what you are reading on your unit will help materially as you learn about mid-depth sonar signals.

bass, bream, crappie, white bass, etc. You probably will lose most of your jig inventory to treetops at first, so pop for the cost of several cards filled with them. You can maximize the fun you are about to have by using ultra-light tackle.

Tie on a jig and go hunting for a strong sonar signal which appears on your unit at mid-depth somewhere. Either

Write notes on your chart paper when you correctly identify an object below. Use these notes to study and review at home until a pattern emerges for you.

drop over a marker buoy on the spot, or use your hard-won skills in turning the boat back to the signal. When you see the signal again on your unit, work the jig down there until you catch whatever it happens to be.

Maybe you'll catch a treetop and lose the jig. If so, take a close look at how that treetop appears on your flasher

or graph. If you are using a graph, write the word ''treetop'' by the image on the paper. If you are using a flasher, do your best to remember how the thing looks in lights. The same procedure applies if you catch a white bass, crappie, bream, etc. Write the word, or remember what the signals look like if you can. Sometimes the signals will be from a school of shad, and you will not catch anything.

The learning process for mid-depth image interpretation is greatly enhanced if you have a graph. You can write

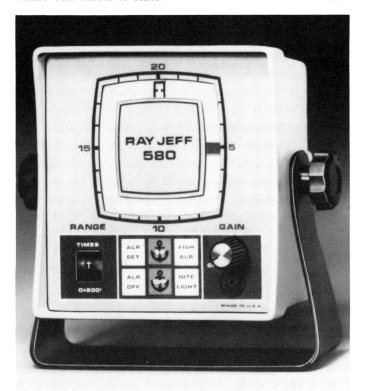

Ray Jeff Model 580 was designed with full feature microprocessor circuitry.

all over the paper as you go, and you can retain the chart paper for reference and comparisons. After several rolls of paper burned in the process, you will begin to observe patterns followed by various species of fish. You will note that trees are usually attached to the bottom of the lake and that shad bunch so tightly together in a school that they appear as a solid mass. (They look that way on a flasher, too.) Crappie seem to school in a somewhat horizontal formation, while white bass position themselves in schools vaguely resembling the shape of a Christmas tree when it is not feeding on the surface. Largemouth bass school much more loosely, and individual "hooks" or arched images are drawn for each fish on the paper. You can't miss the stripers because of their size.

I can't promise the above procedures will enable you to identify correctly the species of every school of fish you see on your depthfinder. I haven't quite mastered that little trick yet myself. (And neither has anybody else!) But by using small jigs to catch and identify the things you see on your sonar equipment, you'll eliminate a whole bunch of hours spent wondering and asking, "What the heck is *that*?"

Phase Two

The majority of sonar operators never progress beyond the basics you have just read over. In fact, I think a respectable percentage of depthfinder users would be delighted with the ability to identify a treetop when they see it on their units. This is said with absolutely no intention to downplay their mental astuteness. But it does reflect the way most of us shy away from hard work in our leisure-time hours.

It takes dedication if you hope to use sonar signals to the fullest extent possible in your fishing.

If you have spent the required time to learn the basic interpretation skills previously covered, and can identify bottom structure, treetops and suspended schools of fish, *and* if you are willing to spend a lot more time learning through personal experience, we shall proceed to more advanced sonar reading techniques.

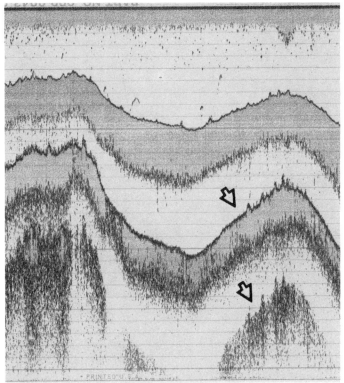

*When the unit's sensitivity is set properly, passing over
a very hard bottom will generate multiple echoes.*

Candidly, what I say here will have to be fortified with
your own experience on the water before much of it will
become clear to you. Possibly, you will choose to take one
situation at a time from the several which follow, and try to
duplicate it several times before proceeding to the next one.

Bottom Composition. Remembering what we said
about the basic principles of sonar, you know that hard

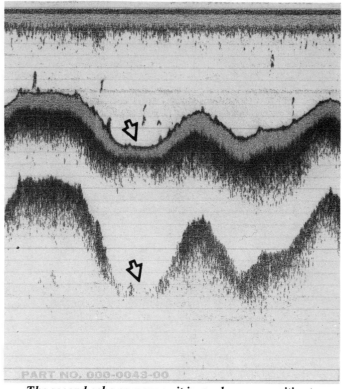

The second echo on your unit is much more sensitive to small changes in bottom composition than the first one. Note as the boat passes over this softer section of bottom the grayline narrows slightly, but the second echo disappears completely.

surfaces reflect more of the signal from your unit than do softer ones. As the transducer passes over a rocky bottom, the flasher signal will become noticeably wider and more intense (brighter). The correct bottom depth remains that of the top part of the signal on the dial. On graph units the bottom also expands, again only in a downward fashion. If your graph has a grayline feature, you will notice the shaded area extends further down on the paper, indicating the hard bottom below. A second or even a third bottom echo will appear on both units, provided the sensitivity is set properly (and there is sufficient room on the graph paper).

Finding an old roadbed hideout for your quarry becomes "a piece of cake" with this knowledge. Finding a submerged weed bed or moss bed is equally easy when you think about it. The signals *weaken* substantially when being absorbed by the vegetation, and the second echo disappears.

Gravel, rock, mud, sand and moss bottoms are all fairly easy to pick out with practice when you watch the returning bottom signals get wider or weaker. Even very slight changes in bottom composition will be shown plainly by the action of the *second* echo. The second bottom echo is much weaker than the first one, so it will be affected far greater by changes in the strength of reflected signals than the initial reading. That's important to remember, especially with flasher units.

Drop-offs. An uneven bottom which climbs or drops irregularly beneath the boat will generate a wide returning signal on your flasher. Actually, it is returning several bottom signals all at once because there are a variety of depths to choose from while going up or down the drop-off. Not being picky, the depthfinder will display all of them for you within the cone from the transducer. Very steep drop-offs show themselves in very wide bottom readings; gradual slopes or drop-offs produce only slightly-enlarged bottom readings.

Nice, smooth slopes on the bottom with no breaks and brush will appear as a solid line on your sonar unit. Rocky

drop-offs will give nervous signals for bottom readings, bouncing the sound waves all around the place to ricochet in every direction. Drop-offs featuring stumps, brush and irregular structure formations will provide broken bottom readings, also.

A flasher can mislead you a bit under these circumstances if you fail to realize what is going on down there. When the transducer is positioned over a slope, especially a steep one, the center of the cone is shooting and receiving signals which strike the bottom at different depths. However, the edge of that cone is weaker than the center with regard to signals. Frequently there seems to be a small, weaker signal hovering just above the main bottom readings at the most shallow point. It looks very much like a fish signal. Usually, it is not.

The single, weaker signal displayed immediately above the bottom readings on a slope is probably an additional returning signal from the bottom. It comes from the outer edge of the cone slightly further up the hillside, and looks like a fish hovering there. This type false reading happens only on a drop-off, and only when the slope is reasonably sharp. When you run over a flat bottom with your flasher unit, the outer edge signals will appear merged into the main bottom reading, although they actually show up *below* the correct depth.

Finally, even the real experts with sonar equipment cannot readily identify fish holding along the bottom on a rocky drop-off. The fish signals simply merge right into the bottom reading. Turning the sensitivity either ''up'' or ''down'' does not help because of the hard, rocky bottom.

There is a slight chance you might be able to spot fish under these conditions, but only if the fish are moving. If there is no wind nor current, and you can sit there without

Credit: Techsonic Industries, Inc.

moving, then it follows that signals which pass through the cone probably come from restless fish. Bottom signals will remain reasonably steady, excluding that little false return mentioned above. The weak bottom signal which hovers above the drop-off will be much less intense than fish signals, although both type signals may come and go.

I'm not sure it's really worth all that time and effort to remain frozen over a rocky drop-off waiting for a fish to swim under the boat. If you want to find out about the

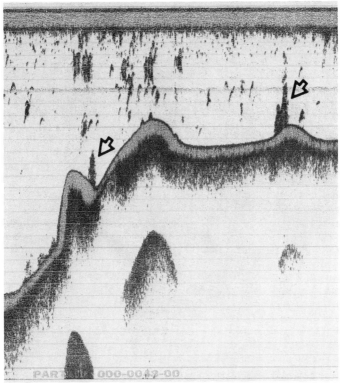

Typical images returning from trees underwater will appear to be firmly attached to the bottom.

presence of fish on the drop, use one of those small jigs. Rocks don't eat jigs in the same manner that fish do.

Brush, Trees and Weeds. Even experienced sonar operators sometimes get fooled, causing them to spend a few minutes fishing for treetops which looked like fish to them. Many times, the signals displayed, especially on a flasher, can look alike.

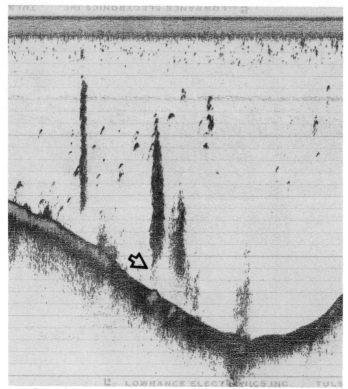

Sometimes, these tree images appear to be "free-floating" in the water, probably because the upper-most limbs are blocking signals, preventing them from reaching the lower portion of the tree.

As a general rule of thumb, you can count on trees and brush to be *attached* to the bottom. Signals for this type structure normally begin at the bottom reading and continue upward in a broken pattern until they reach the top of the underwater object. Unfortunately, it doesn't work exactly like that *every* time on either flashers or graphs.

My boat is equipped with three pretty fancy sonar machines: a pair of flashers and a graph unit. Yet many times I have noticed tall underwater trees which appear to be free-floating when the boat passes over them. At least that's how they look on the depthfinder. I feel the reason for this is due to the mass of branches and limbs which logically extend out from the tree trunk in all directions. These limbs must have the effect of blocking signals, returning all of them back to the transducer before any have traveled the full distance to the base of the tree itself. It's only a theory, but it's the only explanation I can come up with at the moment, too.

In this situation, you will get a complete bottom reading because of the signals going and coming from the edge of the cone. The manner in which a depthfinder displays images makes it appear you are getting a bottom reading directly under the ''suspended'' tree, when you actually are not. As a result, the depthfinder shows an accurate reading for the top two-thirds of the tree height perhaps, shows nothing for the lower portion of the trunk because no signals traveled that far, and gives me a slightly deeper bottom reading than actual.

I believe you can prove this by looking at the signals reflected from a tree as you approach it on the water. Initially, when the tree is being hit by signals on the forward edge of your cone, the angle is better, and the signals can sneak in under some of the branches. You probably observe the tree attached, or perhaps almost attached to the bottom. Then as you move into position more directly above the tree, the thing seems to come up in depth toward you slightly, as if it took a deep breath and floated up a few feet or yards!

Turning up the sensitivity can *sometimes* provide a top-to-bottom reading in these cases, depending on just how tightly massed the limbs are and how much moss is growing on them. Luckily, most of the trees in your lake should provide a complete reading, appearing firmly planted into the bottom.

Using the basics of sonar interpretation will allow you to pull off some pretty nifty tricks with which to impress your fishing partner. For example, you can spot *fish holding inside* the branches of a treetop if you think about it. Hard surfaces reflect more intense returning signals than soft surfaces, right? So if you are over a treetop and turn *down* the sensitivity on your unit, the weak signals from soft, water-soaked branches will fade out. The stronger signals from fish will remain!

Just turn down the sensitivity until the tree signals almost disappear completely. The remaining signals should be coming from fish living there. Of course, getting those fish into your boat from within the treetop sanctuary is still another problem. But if you make a friendly little wager with your fishing pal that you can show him fish *inside* a treetop, you'll probably not have to pay for the beer that day anyway.

Weeds growing upwards from the bottom will return weaker, paler signals than practically any other type surface. Again, using the basics, you can see fish holding in the weed beds easily. No adjustment of sensitivity will be required for that one.

Phase Three

There are still a few advanced techniques to be examined in learning about sonar equipment. You will find with time and experience that your depthfinder becomes the most valuable tool for finding fish which has ever been invented since the Game and Fish boys outlawed fishing with dynamite. As you continue working with your unit(s) on the water, and sharpen your skills for interpreting what the signals represent, you are going to become more aware of subtle differences, small details you never looked for before, and a host of little things which are puzzling.

Some of the more expensive and sophisticated graphs on the market today have an amazing capacity for showing these small readings. By judicious use of the sensitivity control, you can observe where the thermocline is located in the water. As you probably know, the thermocline represents the most productive layer of water for fishing under most conditions. Above it is the epilimnion or surface layer of water which absorbs heat from the sun. Below the thermocline is the hypolimnion, a layer of water with very low oxygen content and usually devoid of fish life.

The reason your graph can show the location of the thermocline hinges upon the rather abrupt temperature change between layers in the water. Sudden temperature changes in the water are accompanied by sudden changes in density. It is that change in water density that the sophisticated units can spot for you, thus telling you the depth of the fish's "comfort zone." That knowledge can be used to advantage.

There are a few built-in errors, or at least illusions, in the sonar readout you see. Fish which can be seen anywhere within the circular cone of sound from your transducer will appear on the face of your unit as if they were directly beneath the boat. Purely by examining the possibilities, you realize that only a very few fish swimming within a given circle will be located exactly in the center of that circle. Percentage-wise, the vast majority of fish you see displayed on your sonar unit will be physically located off to one side or the other, not smack under your transducer as they appear to be. For this reason, most of the fish you see will be from five to ten per cent closer to the surface of the water than they seem to be when displayed on your equipment.

A fish (or any other underwater object) directly under the transducer will be recorded accurately at its exact depth

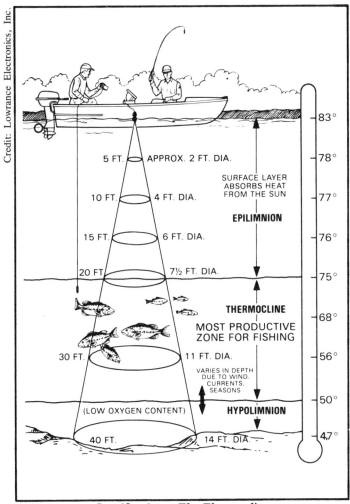

Credit: Lowrance Electronics, Inc.

Stratification – The Thermocline
Many lakes stratify into three distinct layers during
summer months. The thermocline is the layer of water
usually of the greatest interest to fishermen because it
provides the water temperatures most fish prefer.

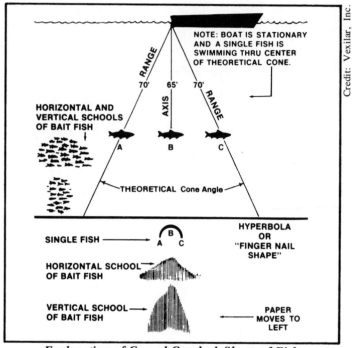

Explanation of Curved Graphed Shape of Fish

on your depthfinder. If he is near the edge of the sound cone, and thereby further away from the transducer, he will appear to be deeper in the water because of the additional time lapse required for the signal to reach him and be received back.

Perhaps the easiest way to see this mechanical function of sonar is to take a look at the hooked, or "arched" figures drawn on a graph. When a suspended fish first enters the circle of sound waves from your transducer as the boat moves along, he is at his furthest distance away from the transducer in that circle. When your unit initially records the

Humminbird's LCR 4000 video is capable of a total screen update, both when changing depth ranges or zooming in detail, has stop-action and reverse.

fish signal for you, he is on the outer edge of the cone. As you continue to approach the fish, the reflected signal takes less time to return to your machine because you are getting closer to the fish. This is why the arch drawn for a fish on your graph starts at the bottom and moves upward as you get closer. The distance to the fish has decreased, so the signal is printed closer to the water surface. As you pass over the fish, the arch peaks, and begins to be drawn in a downward direction until the fish passes out of the sound cone. The arch reaches its highest point on the graph paper when the fish is at its closest location to the transducer.

The *actual* depth of the fish will be shown as the highest part of the arch, but *only* if the fish is directly below the transducer when you pass over it. We're talking in terms of

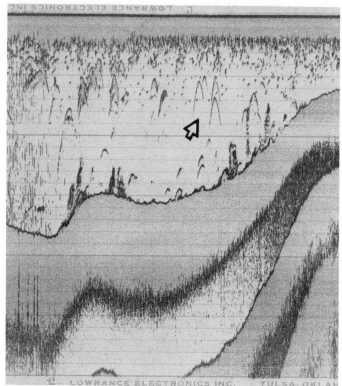

*On your graph unit, fish signals which are drawn with
a sharply pointed arch are from fish directly
under the transducer.*

only a matter of inches here if you are fishing in most
freshwater lakes. But there is a very practical advantage to
knowing these facts.

With your graph, you can quickly determine if the fish
you see are truly under the boat or if they are off to one side.
This "fine point" in interpretation can make a substantial

More gentle, rounded arches are drawn for fish located off to the side of the boat.

difference in your success when vertical jigging for suspended fish which are tightly bunched. The more sharply the arch is formed, the closer the fish is to being directly under the transducer. The lazy, gentle arches you see are caused by fish passing through the outer edges of the cone. Their signals are more rounded in appearance on the graph because they do not make as great a change in their relative position to the transducer. Sharp arches mean fish under the transducer. Rounded arches mean fish off to the side.

Generally speaking, the larger the image on your depthfinder, the larger the fish it is showing. This is true enough for single fish swimming through the cone of your transducer. But when two or more fish are swimming very close together, you may get a merger of their signals, presenting a "larger than life" image. Also, when two or more fish are passing beneath your transducer at the same depth, although they may be several feet apart horizontally, your unit may well display their signals as one. Signals are blended and merged into one, because the fish are at the same depth. This is especially true with flasher units.

Another funny-looking image which pops up on graphs frequently is a thin, straight vertical line, often seeming to be floating in the water. The recorded signal looks as if you just passed over a half-floating telephone pole, and can stretch for several feet in height as shown on the chart paper. Sometimes this phenomenon appears as a series of small arches stacked one on top of the other for several feet top-to-bottom. As no variety of man nor fish I can think of stacks itself tightly in single file vertically underwater, what could this signal represent on your graph?

Air bubbles or escaping gas from the bottom seems the only reasonable answer.

Conclusions

We began this section by saying nothing can substitute for personal experience in gaining expertise for reading sonar signals. As you have gathered by now, that expertise requires long hours of serious study on the water. I have logged several thousand hours on the lakes with my depth-

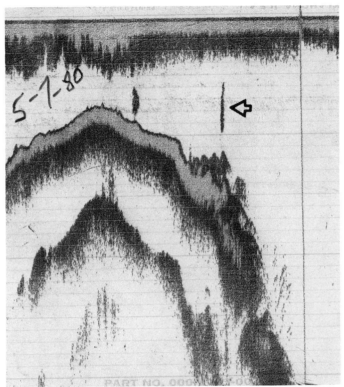

Occasional images on a graph which appear as straight vertical lines suspended in the water, and covering several feet in height, are likely caused by air bubbles and escaping gas from the bottom.

finders running while I studied them. And I still learn things as I continue. I also wonder "What the heck is *that*?" from time to time.

You cannot bolt on a depthfinder, run to the water and triple your fishing success immediately. Do not allow frus-

Author displays nice bass taken vertical jigging after finding active fish with sonar.

tration to make you impatient. You *will* increase your fishing success dramatically as you gain experience and apply it to your technique for boating fillets. I don't recommend you volunteer to supply the main course for the church fish fry two weeks after your first sonar purchase, unless you already have the little devils in your freezer.

Learn to read bottom detail first. Use a topo map as an aid whenever possible. When you are satisfied with your ability to identify drop-offs, trees, underwater islands, etc., begin working on fish signals. If you have a graph, don't fail to write notes on the paper explaining what you find. Small jigs are quite valuable in learning how to read fish signals.

As you master the basics of interpretation, your personal skills and ingenuity will begin to take part in the learning process. You will build expertise with depthfinders in direct relation to the time and effort you are willing to give. If you get too frustrated, go back to Square One and start over with the basics again.

You can master sonar interpretations. If you want to badly enough.

You have worked pretty hard with your unit(s) so far (hopefully not just reading) and it's time to put things to the test. The next section will provide tips and techniques for catching several popular species of fish. As I relate a few past experiences, you should be able to see where sonar equipment plays a major role in fishing success. At least that's the whole idea.

5

Time To Go Fishing

Big Bass, Little Bass

I arrived in Houston with a flourish. Rain was dancing on the runway as I thanked God for letting the wings on the plane not fall off until I was safely back to earth. Having never been overly fond of flying, I was too elated to have my feet back on something that did not dip, plunge and shudder, to notice the joyous faces all around me in the airport.

People were saying things like "Isn't it wonderful! We haven't had rain like this in months!" I paid little heed, thinking they were laughing at the greenish tint to my complexion. Besides, my eardrums were still turned inside-out from the cabin pressure.

The cab driver took up where the people in the luggage area left off, repeating praise for the stuff that had soaked my canvas baggage while it sat outside for 30 minutes on one of those little funny carts they use to unload jets. I needed a hot bath and a drink, not necessarily in that order.

The thought of putting on clean, wet underwear was less than thrilling.

About eight dollars before we reached my motel room in Conroe, I began to notice the sky. Thick, grayish-black clouds were massed in a solid wall-to-wall blanket overhead. I made a mental note to get the name of the pilot who had been able to find Houston in that mess. Perhaps I would mention him in my will.

The rain continued for three days. The fish in Lake Conroe *had* been attacking everything you could reasonably tie onto monofilament, and I had gone there on assignment by one of the major outdoor magazines to document the fun with professional fisherman, Rick Clunn. Clunn is a very likeable chap and had won back-to-back world championships for his ability to catch bass. He gave me a dandy interview on my tape recorder as we sat by the window watching it rain. But even he couldn't make the wet go away.

Another lad, named Randy Fite, had agreed to take me fishing on Lake Conroe during my stay there. Fite was alleged to be something of a wonder in the use of depthfinders. He, too, gave me a dandy indoor interview which was only slightly affected on tape by the pounding of water on the roof.

A few days later, and only hours before my motel bill became totally ridiculous, the rain stopped. Fite and I dashed to the lake, jumped into his boat and scooted away to one of his pet fishing holes. I covered my camera with a jacket to protect it from the soggy air.

I'm sure you know what happens when a few tons of water fall into a lake after a dry spell. Old shorelines are replaced by new ones. Productive structure suddenly becomes too deep beneath the surface. Water temperature

*Randy Fite showed me how to tell if a bass would bite
or not before wetting the hook.*

changes. And the water gets muddy. It always gets muddy.

"We're gonna have to hunt for them, Buck," Randy said after viewing what had been one of his favorite fishing holes only days earlier.

And hunt we did. Within minutes, Fite had located bass with his depthfinder graph. I found an almost dry spot to put my camera, set my can of wonder tonic on the deck and grabbed for my fishing rod. Fite shook his head.

"Those aren't active bass," he said casually. "They would be tough to catch. Let's go find another bunch.

"Don't forget about your beer can," he said, pushing the throttle forward as I stared in utter disbelief.

We ran a few miles up the lake to another spot. The

graph pinpointed more little arches and Randy smiled. To me, these fish images looked just like the first set. But not to Randy. He dropped the trolling motor over and eased the boat back into position. We began catching bass almost at once. When the action slowed, he cranked the engine and went hunting again.

Every time the man said we were going to catch bass, one or both of us did exactly that. It was a miracle. I remember thinking that jet pilot didn't have anything on Fite.

I fished with Randy the following day, also. This time he let me challenge his expertise, although my ego would have been better off if he had not. I spent hours casting at bass he said were "inactive," and caught a total of two fish. We caught five at the first stop where *he* wanted to fish.

Until it was proven to me rather forcefully, I seriously doubted Fite's statement that you could look at bass on a graph depthfinder and determine if they would bite or not. He made a believer of me that day in Conroe, and I have since proved it many times in my own boat.

There is a definite pattern to the way bass behave when they are feeding (active) and when they are suspended (inactive). The differences between the two types of behavior are easily seen on a good graph. They do act in a predictable fashion which you can use in catching more of them because of your image burner. Your ability to *see* how they look down there will do wonderful things for the weight of your stringer.

When a bass begins to feed, he approaches structure in the water. The structure is holding the menu upon which he is about to dine. He will actually come into physical contact with that structure in his efforts to gobble minnows and crayfish living there. Conversely, when the bass has his belly full and wants nothing more than to relax, daydream

*Very loosely schooled bass like these, suspended away
from structure are accurately classed "inactive."*

or rest peacefully, he pulls a short distance away from the
structure and suspends. It's reasonable to assume you will
catch more bass when they are hungry and feeding than you
will by chunking hardware at them while they sit around
dormant with a full tummy. How the bass relates physically
to the structure tells you when those short periods of activity
are about to fill your ice chest.

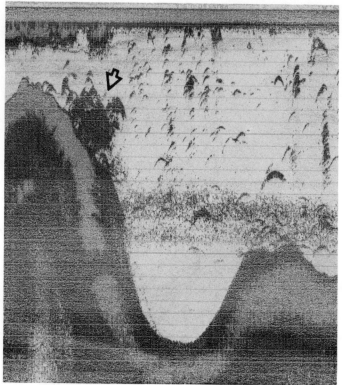

When bass school tightly and move into physical
contact with the structure, they are actively feeding
and **highly** *catchable.*

You can see when the bass come into contact with the
structure simply by watching where the arches appear on the
paper. When the fish signals on your graph are several feet
away from the structure, the fish are going to be uncoopera-
tive at best. You can run to another part of the lake and hope
the fish over there are following a different bus schedule. It

is wise to continue checking back on the inactive school you have found from time to time. They gotta eat sooner or later.

Another tip-off about how feeding bass appear on your graph comes from the way they school together. Inactive bass avoid conversation with others. But as bass begin to feed, they bunch much more tightly together. This is probably a bit of the old killer instinct in them. A wolf pack in the north woods bands together and uses teamwork to down a caribou. Bass probably have some of that same predator ingenuity when chasing stuff they like to eat.

Using a graph, you can observe how bass relate to structure, and you can tell if they are going to bite readily or not. It's true. Interestingly enough, when water conditions get pretty lousy down deep, and the bass have to live several feet above the structure, it still works. They suspend off to one side above the structure they are relating to; when they begin to feed, they move directly over it.

I began fishing for bass with a high school chum named Raymond Dismukes. We lived in South Georgia, and the proper way to catch bass at that time was to go fishing twice. The first trip was made with tiny doughballs or small red "coffee" worms if we could save enough pennies to buy them. Our first afternoon was spent catching shiners. Big shiners that were fun to play with in the water on a limber cane pole. The second day was spent feeding the shiners to the bass.

Now, in the eyes of my friend, "deep water" was anything he couldn't walk through without getting his shoulders wet. We had a swimming hole at the river with a big length of rope tied to a high branch in an oak tree. And, all us kids loved to go skinny dipping in the river, taking turns swinging on the rope out over the water, letting go at the maximum height of some six or seven feet, and screaming as loudly as possible while dropping into the water. The water was about six feet deep where we made our ungainly entry, and the whole process was a hell of a lot more fun than Algebra II.

Raymond never knew the joys of that rope swing over the river. We all figured (correctly) that he couldn't swim, but never teased him about it. He was considerably bigger than the rest of us at the time.

Many years later when I moved to Tennessee and learned a few things about using depthfinders to locate bass, I invited Raymond to come for a visit. We would go bass fishing and I would demonstrate all the fantastic things I had learned with sonar. Raymond brought his shiner bucket with him.

With all due respect to the folks who manufacture life vests, I was unable to get Raymond in the boat. After some fair amount of conversation, it was decided we would have a "fish-off." Raymond would use the shiners he spotted in the live bait tank at the marina, and I would use whatever I chose in the boat. He stayed on the bank. I went out in the lake to the old river channel. (Raymond was disgruntled because the dock operator wouldn't let him fish for shiners in the bait tank, saying that was half the fun anyway.)

Having waited until mid-summer to invite Raymond for a visit, there was no apparent way he could catch more bass in shallow water than I could on the old river channel. Fortunately, that's the way it worked out. He took one look at the limit of bass I brought in later, and we made plans for him to fish with me in the boat the following morning!

Whether he can swim or not, the average bass fisherman seems to define "deep water" for his pursuits as anything over 10 or 11 feet. In the spring and fall, this love for shallow water can be quite productive. A guy tools along the shoreline tossing a variety of lures at shallow structure, and he scores. But in either winter or summer, the fish seem to prefer deeper houses. It is at these times that your sonar gear will really shine.

I must admit having little luck at catching bass below the 25-foot mark. However, I have boated a respectable number that were at depths close to that, and holding around an underwater island surrounded by *really* deep liquid. Your ability to find these island "humps" in the lake comes from sonar use. And while it is true that bass are found more shallow in spring and fall, you can motor out to where an old creek bed enters the lake and find excellent action many times. I have caught braggin' size bass out away from shore when everybody else was coming back to the dock to describe the action in knee-deep water.

My point is, don't let your idea of bass fishing revolve around shallow water only, regardless of how you define what is "shallow or deep." Your sonar equipment has limited use in the real shallow stuff because it can only cover a very small portion of the bottom at close range.

If you haven't experienced the fun of catching bass suspended over deep structure in winter or summer, you have missed a lot of action!

Fall is one of my favorite times for bass fishing. You can find them in both shallow and deep water, and as a bonus, the larger bass are becoming active again after a long, lazy summer. Accurate use of depthfinders at this time of year can produce spectacular success by allowing you to concentrate your work in productive water.

Regarding shallow-water efforts, creek channels are prime places to fish. You might begin out at the mouth of the creek where water is about 10 to 12 feet deep on the shoulder of the channel, tapering down to perhaps 20 to 25 feet in the channel itself. Using your sonar to stay on course, begin working the channel banks systematically as you progress up the creek. Bass don't always hold right on the lip of the channel, but they stay pretty close during this period.

A lead spoon is quite effective for working out a creek channel. It gets to the bottom quickly and is easy to cast. Bounce it on the lip and let it fall into the channel. Make the lure "hop" a couple of times, then repeat the procedure. You can use the depthfinder to "crisscross" the channel with the boat, finding structure and staying in the productive area.

Creeks filled with brush might best be worked with shallow-running crank baits. Run the lure just deep enough to clear the top of the brush. You are trying to locate the fish at this point, not fill the ice chest, so use a lure that works efficiently in the structure encountered. When you find those fish, then you can switch over to another more deliberate technique which may work better.

As you get further back into the creek, switch to a smaller size crank bait, worm, jig, etc. Usually, the bass found way back in the creek during fall will be smaller than those still out near the main lake where the water is deeper. If you have several below-freezing nights all of a sudden, as sometimes happens in fall, you may have to switch to a *real* tiny bait. Fast-dropping water temperatures will clobber those fish in shallow places. Their metabolism will slow down to approximate a state of shock, and it will take *very* small baits worked *very* slowly to get them.

Another good spot for finding fall bass is a moss bed, practically anywhere in the lake you can find one. Bass love these things, and the action can be excellent at almost any time of day. Here again, use the lure that seems best suited for the initial encounter with the bass. Crank baits would likely stay fouled most of the time; so would spoons. Spinnerbaits would be an ideal choice for use in searching for bass around moss beds. The plastic worm would work well, also, but it might be pretty slow if you have a large area to cover.

Cover the moss bed completely. Work the lure all around the outside edges, over the top and in the middle where there are pockets. Bass could be holding practically anywhere in the structure. They *could* be just sitting off to one side admiring it.

Rock and rip-rap will hold a surprising number of bass in the fall months, too. The best method for fishing that type structure is to position your boat near the edge and cast up or down the shoreline, bringing the lure back parallel to it. Crank baits or spinnerbaits produce well, worked from one to five feet away from the edge.

During an interview with bass fishing pro, Rick Clunn, he gave me some points to remember about fall bass fishing. Rick breaks down fall fishing into two parts: "early fall" and "late fall." This is due to the possible changes in the oxygen levels you find in so many lakes at this time of year. For example, the month of September can still be considered part of summer in some areas, and the lake may well have bad oxygen in the deep water areas. This puts more fish up shallow, obviously. In November, the oxygen usually is good back down to the 18 to 25-foot range, and many

Rick Clunn is one of the country's finest professional fishermen, and he relies heavily upon his depthfinders for success.

bass will move back out in the lake to deeper structure. Water temperatures have a lot to do with this, although Clunn doesn't pattern his fishing around water temperature.

He patterns his fishing around a number of things, but one of the most important is what he sees on his depthfinders.

Your alternate choice for bass fishing in the fall is deep water, generally considered to be water between 15 and 30 feet. In this situation, the distinction between early and late season is even more critical. Oxygen levels can still be bad in most warm climate areas, causing fish out in the main lake to be suspended over structure instead of down on it. Suspended bass are usually harder to catch, and the vertical jigging technique which often works best is tough to master.

The plus side of deep water fall fishing comes from your ability to use your depthfinder to cover a great deal of water accurately without ever wetting a line. You never even have to cut off your boat's engine until after you have found fish. The procedure is to motor from one deep-water structure to the next, checking each spot for fish. If they are on the structure, you can see them with sonar. If not, you merely drive to the next place. There is no point fishing unproductive water, and once you have learned to read your depthfinder well, you can cover a sizeable chunk of the lake without wasting time.

For this fishing, it helps to have both a flasher and a graph in the boat. You run to the structure using the flasher, then check out the action with your graph. *Once you have gained the skills for finding active bass before you shut down the big engine on the boat, your fishing success in deep water will improve fantastically!*

Ideally, you might have a *third* depthfinder in the boat. This one would be in the bow, the transducer mounted on

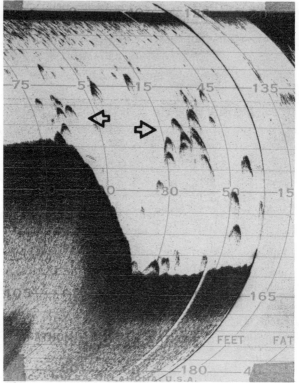

This example of schooling bass was recorded on a curve-line graph, and shows either the beginning or the end of a feeding spree. Note the bass schooled loosely at the right, suspended away from the structure. Fish on the left are more tightly grouped and are in contact with the structure. It is possible the bass on the left are still feeding (and can be caught easily) while the others have finished their meal and drifted out to rest. Of course, those active fish could be the "early birds," and that means the whole bunch will be over there feeding actively in a couple of minutes!

the trolling motor. Once active bass have been located, the trolling motor sonar unit allows you to stay directly on top of the fish. Vertical jigging requires accurate lure presentation for success.

Having never read any of today's fishing magazines, your depthfinder cannot tell the difference between a 15-inch bass and a 15-inch carp. It displays both equally on the face of your unit, so it becomes your job to tell the difference between bass and other species. But in the case of a single fish of moderate size, you won't know purely by looking at his picture on sonar. You have to use your knowledge of fish habitat to help figure it out. A single fish out in deep water away from structure will probably not be a bass.

Vertical fishing with a spoon, grub or plastic worm is quite effective. You must place the offering accurately in the productive zone where the fish are, and the difference can be only a matter of a yard or so in cold weather. If the fish show up on your unit at 20 feet below the surface, working your bait several feet above or below the school won't do much for your reputation as an expert. And many times, deep water bass group together tightly, making it possible for the guy in the bow of the boat to get action with almost every drop, while the dude in the back never gets a hit!

Most strikes, maybe 90 per cent, while vertical jigging will come as the lure drops or flutters downward. You can't afford to have slack in your line at that critical moment, so after you "hop" or pull the lure upwards, catch it there with your line. Then follow the lure back down by lowering your rod, keeping the line tight. If you establish a set rhythm for doing this, you'll notice instantly any variation in the way the line acts. Even if you don't feel the fish strike, a twitch or slight pause in the line tells you a fish has hit, and you set the hook immediately.

Deep-water bass fishing is both fun and productive, although most people never try it seriously. Learn to use your depthfinders well and you'll find this method for taking bass is deadly.

Crappie Any Time You Want Them

I have probably written more magazine articles on the subject of fishing for crappie than any other species. They are pegged the number one fish in popularity here in my home state of Tennessee, and may well enjoy similar notoriety where you live. Crappie are predictable in their movements, and while the average angler may consider them as a "one month species," crappie can be caught handily in every month of the year.

If you know how to use a depthfinder, that is.

It was after some 20 years of catching crappie from the bank in April that I bought my first sonar unit. I had owned a little johnboat for many years prior, but it was used for bass and bream fishing, an activity that consumed my every weekend and almost cost me my job a couple of times on Thursdays. That was back in the dark days when I worked as an accountant to earn a steady paycheck.

Finding crappie with a depthfinder never even entered my mind. Crappie were mystery fish which magically came into shore sometime in early spring, attacked minnows if they were swimming beneath a red-and-white cork float,

A great many people think the only time to catch crappie is when the dogwood trees are blooming. Sonar expertise makes year-around fun available.

and then disappeared again into the unknown from whence they had come.

A chap named Waldo Blake used to enjoy stopping by the house on Wednesday evenings in those days. I am positive it was the only night of the week his wife would let him out of the house, and then it was for the purpose of going bowling. Waldo didn't know one end of a bowling ball from the other, and didn't care to learn. He always brought a bottle of Vodka to the house with him.

Now, old Waldo had heard me talk about fishing ever since we met. Actually, more than a few of the times I got my behind in a sling for missing work to go fishing on Thursdays, it was due to making plans the night before under the effect of Waldo's liquid inspiration.

Well, it so happened that about the time I bought my new depthfinder, Waldo's wife went for a rare two-week visit with her mother in another state. Waldo honored me highly by deciding to spend his first weekend of freedom in 12 years fishing in my boat. Monday morning after that particular weekend of festivities, my own wife left for an undetermined period of time, indicating she would return shortly after Waldo's wife did, or the day Waldo ceased to spend his nights sleeping on our living room floor, whichever came first.

One sunny afternoon, I can't remember now if it was on that first weekend or one of the vacation days I took immediately following it, Waldo and I caught a crappie. He had taken a swipe with his hat at a school of minnows on the surface by the boat. He missed, but the wave action flipped one over the side of the johnboat where it jumped and flopped until he grabbed it to put on his hook. We had been fishing with medium-size, five-inch bass shiners, trying to catch what appeared to be a large school of bass on the depthfinder. Moments after Waldo's minnow reached the school, a crappie took it. It was the Great New Beginning in my crappie fishing. And I don't think Waldo ever knew what happened. He tried to net it with his hat, and the fish got away.

He smiled, took another little taste from the remaining bottle, and said, "Pale-looking brim, wasn't it? Bass musta just spit him out!"

In the years that passed, sonar equipment got better, and so did my success with crappie fishing in months other than April. I found that you could follow crappie around the lake as they migrate from one location preference to another. There is a definite pattern to their movements on the lakes and creeks where I have tried this, and I'll wager you can plot the same kind of info on your local water. Their timetable can change with climate and between sections of the country. Here is what they do in Tennessee and Kentucky; adjust the dates slightly for your own area if necessary.

In the really cold months like January and February, crappie are usually found near the deep water out around major entrances to large coves in the lake. They do not feed actively at this time of year, probably using all their extra energy to keep the fire going. They require little food for survival as their metabolism has slowed materially.

Toward the end of February and the first part of March, crappie begin to migrate toward shore. They leave the deeper water and head into the mouths of creeks. The first place they stop is on the high ridges in that area. They are congregating here, and are rather plentiful when you find them. "Hot spots" for action frequently are on these ridges where deep water is adjacent to them. On warmer days you can enjoy excellent fishing there.

Crappie stay on those high ridges near the mouths of creeks for many days, sometimes for weeks. Early March fishing requires a light touch to detect the faint bite typical of cold water. The fish often merely take the minnow into their mouth and hold it there. You may even have to raise your pole from time to time to see if a fish is on the other end. (If your friends thought your home movies were boring when they featured your two kids and your funny bird dog, don't waste film on this type crappie fishing action.) Cold-water crappie do taste better, though. The meat is firmer. And you usually have the lake to yourself.

When April comes around the crappie begin leaving the ridges, looking for a handy spot at which to accomplish their brief love affairs. They go in closer to shore, seeking wooden structure of some sort: treetops, stumps, brush, etc. And they scatter all over the place. Typically, if you find brush piles in reasonably shallow water during April, you find the spot occupied by mating crappie. Their activities seem to give them quite an appetite, and you normally have no trouble catching them easily with minnows or jigs.

Immediately following the spawning season, it gets tough trying to find crappie. Reminiscent of the old jokes about rabbits, they seem to say "Thank you, ma'am" and split. You will find good numbers of fish at a particular location one morning, go back to the dock for a sandwich and more minnows, then return only to discover the crappie are gone. They just wander around aimlessly for a month or more after spawning. You are forced to search for them much more with your depthfinder, but when you locate a school, they bite eagerly.

As the water continues to get warmer, crappie begin a full-scale migration back out toward the main lake. Not all crappie migrate out into the main lake. Some of the smaller ones remain closer to shore, perhaps hoping April will come back. But the majority of crappie will leave the shore area. By July they will have established residence along the old river bed.

Contrary to popular thought, when the summer sun is hot enough to make your tennis shoes smell like catfish bait, crappie are the easiest to find and catch regularly. Summertime crappie will definitely be on the old river channel in most large lakes, and if you exercise a bit of patience, you can fill a stringer with them. You are required to find the shoulder of the channel with your depthfinder, then find some structure there. The fish depth can vary, but they are usually between 15 and 25 feet down on the slope into the channel. Once you find the old river channel, you may have several *miles* of productive area to enjoy. And as a bonus, you'll find several other species of fish sharing the same accommodations.

When September appears on the calendar, the fish pack up and migrate again. Both September and October are *excellent* months for crappie fishing fun. They come back into the creek mouths, returning to approximately the same places you found them back in March; i.e., the high spots on ridges. They do not school very tightly at this time, but they stay there for a while instead of wandering again, and when you find them with sonar, you'll have plenty of fun.

As the weather continues to cool down in October, the fish take a step backwards; they move out slightly, back to the entrance of big coves and bays. Again, they take to the high spots which have deep water immediately next door. And they make up their minds to stay there until things get warmer. Crappie stay in those areas all through the winter. Then in late February or early March, they move again, heading for the good times at the shoreline.

Very few fish lend themselves to depthfinder use better than crappie. Their movements are predictable with a good degree of accuracy as they migrate back and forth in the lake, and sonar skills allow you to find their little wet noses with ease. To illustrate the point, consider a magazine assignment I was given to do recently.

Outdoor magazine editors love big name celebrities. They like to get articles featuring the top three or four professional fishermen in the world, or some Million Dollar Baby who smacks baseballs over the fence. They like articles where movie or TV stars can be shown performing some outdoor adventure. And they like Country Music. Well, most of them do.

I have had fun hunting and fishing with a number of top-notch entertainers in the Country Music field. Sometimes it was for a magazine article, sometimes it was just for the fun. We live in a little town close to Nashville, so it is only natural (if you work at it hard enough) to have an occasional opportunity to meet some of these folks.

In the early fall of 1980, I was given an assignment on fall crappie fishing by one fine magazine. As luck would have it, I had spent all summer trying to get photos of some hard-to-snag stripers for several other articles. I had not been crappie fishing in months. And the editor gave me a two-week deadline. As I type slower than a turtle sleeps, and develop pictures in my darkroom only at the eleventh hour because I don't like to do it, I had a slight problem with time. But I agreed to the deadline.

I felt fairly sure I could go to the lake, catch a stringer of crappie, and write the article. But it was dreary outside, the deadline was rushed, and crappie historically do not make good action photos. I needed something to brighten the photos and the text. Quite by accident, I discovered Louise Mandrell likes to go fishing.

There are times in the life of a freelance writer when things go well. These times are few, but this was one of them. Louise agreed to help me out. Arrangements were made for Louise and her husband to meet me at the marina. Being somewhat flawed in character, I decided to catch the fish before she arrived. Just in case. This I accomplished with the assistance of a friend whom I threatened with bodily harm should he hang around when Louise arrived. We caught a perfectly beautiful stringer of nice fall crappie.

The "not so good times" which freelancers must endure,

followed immediately afterwards. Louise and R.C. arrived, and due to their frantic schedule had only about 30 minutes to give me. Heck, it takes me almost that long to focus the dials and knobs on my cameras! (I have a strong distaste for the things, as they never seem to reproduce pictures the way I see them.)

The short time we had together was spent shooting pictures in a misty rain which began four minutes after they drove up at the marina. She posed, held up a stringer of fish for me, and did everything possible a photographer could ask. Trouble was, I am basically a writer, not a camera buff. Louise gave me her time, let me burn three rolls of film on her, stole my heart with a warm smile, and left for California to begin filming their TV series, "Barbara Mandrell and the Mandrell Sisters."

I still did not have a story to write. Picture-taking had consumed all the time. She never *really* went fishing with me, so cursing something which a few writers call "ethics," I called the magazine editor to say I had not been able to get my article. The rain had set in and didn't stop for six days.

Despite my failure in getting the article, the fact my friend and I were able to catch a fine stringer of crappie "on cue," as it were, demonstrates the value of sonar equipment. We caught the fish easily after locating structure in the appropriate part of the lake.

I only wish Louise could have been there with us.

While it is self-evident that crappie move into the shore to spawn during springtime, the activity is not one which can be isolated to an exact date on the calendar. Many a

Previously unused photo of lovely Louise Mandrell.

vacation has been planned months in advance to coincide with the crappie spawning runs, only to discover the action was much better the week before. Or the week after.

During the spring, crappie can be rather unpredictable. This is due in part to the things which affect their daily life. Spring itself, is unpredictable in nature. When the weather breaks, presenting several gorgeous, warm days in a row, the females move into shallow water, preparing to lay their eggs. Then it rains. Or it turns cold and drops the temperature a bit. The females react by retreating into deeper water, playing a "wait-and-see" game.

In bodies of water which eventually flow through a man-made dam, spawning crappie are often influenced by the guy who controls the gates. They may move into the shallow water, find a housesite, and awake the next morning to find the gatekeeper has dropped the lake level several inches. Heavy spring rains often make gatekeepers do things like that. Again, the crappie must back off to reconsider.

Combinations and changes in water level and temperature make it practically impossible to pick the exact date and location for crappie to spawn. The spawning season usually will cover a four-to-six week period, with fish coming and going steadily like picnic ants hot on the trail of a Honey Bun. There can be little doubt of finding crappie near shore in springtime, but exactly *where* they are on a given day is not all that easy to guess. They can be almost anywhere in the general area of the creek mouths. Shallow, deep and suspended.

Depthfinders allow fishermen to locate the underwater structure which crappie like: drop-offs, creek channels, stick-ups, stumps, etc. While bank fishing for spawning crappie is by far the most-used technique, backing your boat out into the open water over this type structure can produce much more consistent success in the spring. For one thing, all crappie do not go to the bank for spawning at the same time. This is why the activity lasts for several weeks. New arrivals are moving in all the time. And they work that off-shore structure *both* coming to and going from the bank. Bank fishing may be unpredictable because of weather conditions, but catching crappie several yards away from shore on structure is a sure bet.

Many experts on crappie fishing are convinced the really *large* crappie spawn in eight to 12-foot water around stumps. Another reason to work water away from the bank.

The most efficient tackle and technique for catching deeper-water crappie was demonstrated to me many years ago on Kentucky Lake. It consists of two hooks spaced about 18 inches apart, with a one or two-ounce lead weight attached to the line either between the hooks or an additional 18 inches below the bottom hook. With a lively minnow on each hook, the procedure is to "walk" or "bounce" the lead weight along the bottom in the structure. You actually can "feel" the structure as the lead weight touches it while you concentrate on keeping a tight line.

Having two hooks spaced apart in this manner, you offer your bait at different levels simultaneously. Strangely, you find most of your fish will hit either one or the other. That small difference in depth can make a material difference. Of course, you catch two crappie at the same time on occasion. Thin wire hooks are used because the procedure naturally involves getting hung on the structure. With practice, you learn to raise and lower your pole gently when the rig gets hung on something. The lead weight usually will dislodge the tangled hook as it drops back downward. If this fails, you can pull straight up on the line, and the thin hooks

*Crappie can be caught handily in every month of the
year, even August.*

will straighten out, releasing the structure.

Sensitive poles, usually between 10 and 15 feet in
length, work best for the bottom-bumping method. You can
purchase a fiberglass pole designed for this needed sensitivity, use a cane pole with a good tip, or convert your old fly
rod into a crappie-catching tool. It helps greatly to have a
line keeper on the pole. You can wrap excess line around

Credit: Santee Cooper Country

Double-hook crappie rigs are extremely effective.

the spool or cleat, using it later when you enter deeper water and the additional mono is needed to reach bottom.

Tight-line fishing, or "bottom bumping," is fantastically productive on crappie every month of the year. When you feel a fish tap the bait, set the hook immediately; don't wait for him to tote the lead weight off somewhere. I suggest you use at least 15-pound monofilament line for this

technique. You'll need enough line strength to survive
while straightening out the wire hooks which refuse to "jig-
gle" free of brush. And you may need it for landing a much
larger fish that chomps your minnow down there. Tales of
boating big bass and catfish on these crappie rigs are common.

Some professional crappie guides use 40-pound line
for their double-hook rigs. They neither like to waste time
on snags, nor spend the day tying on new terminal tackle for
their customers. If the water you fish is on the cloudy side,
you probably can use the heavy stuff O.K. But if your lake
is fairly clear, you'll catch more fish by using line in the 15
to 20-pound class.

Stripers: The Tackle Busters

When a big striper takes your bait, he is about as subtle
as a trainwreck. One second you're sitting there holding the
rod casually, and the next second you're trying desperately
to keep it in your grasp! Gears in the reel's drag mechanism
are whizzing around audibly, line is disappearing rapidly
from the spool and your rod is being pulled powerfully
downwards. All this happens, of course, only if the fish
failed in his initial attempt to jerk the entire rod and reel out
of your hands and into the water. The sensation is not unlike
having your hook snagged unexpectedly by a nuclear sub
passing below at full tilt.

I have never guided anyone for stripers who did not
utter some kind of whoop or war cry when experiencing
their first-ever encounter with a striper. Usually the sound is
a mixture of fear and astonishment coming from deep in the
stomach. One lady angler I guided on her first striper trip

began screaming bloody murder on the first strike, and continued non-stop until she totally lost her voice. We communicated the remainder of the day using hand signals.

My own initiation to fresh water fury came at approximately the same time I discovered how hard it is to breathe in a bass boat doing 60 mph across the water in March. My local lake, Percy Priest near Nashville, had been stocked with striper fingerlings in 1968. The fish had grown substantially over the years in size, and repeat stocking by the Game and Fish boys increased their numbers annually. I had heard about striper fishing, but had been entirely too busy writing magazine copy and romancing my recent bride to tax my heart further with anything new.

I was talked into an early spring striper trip by a local chap who had been enjoying spectacular action on the lake for years. We met at the dock, backed the boat into partially-thawed water, and headed out into the lake. Robert had not revealed in prior conversations that he had suicidal tendencies, a fact which became evident moments after we cleared the ''No Wake'' buoys.

The huge engine pushed his small, lightweight boat across the lake with breath-taking, eye-watering speed. Add to that the increased wind chill factor on a very cold morning, and you begin to get the picture. I was used to fishing in my johnboat with an 18 hp engine which topped out at around 15 mph. Even so, the excitement which was to follow would rival the boat ride.

We tried casting topwater Redfins over underwater humps and along shoreline ledges. This produced only a few half-hearted swirls a foot or so behind the lure. Robert decided we should troll awhile. This we did, using a deep-running lure with a trailing jig and pork rind. Robert apparently does everything fast. Including trolling.

The stubby boat rod he presented for my use was bending the bones in my left forearm as it strained against the drag from the big lure. Then something grabbed the plug causing the rod to lurch violently toward the transom, taking my white knuckles with it. When both my arms were extended fully, something went pop between my shoulders, and the fight was on.

The 18-pound striper ripped and snorted for what seemed to be an hour, but was more likely in the area of a minute per pound. Robert helped with the oversized net, then collapsed in a fit of laughter, trying to describe my antics while fighting the fish. Then he congratulated me, turned the boat around for another pass, and we did it all over again. The morning ended with four big stripers standing on their heads in the small livewell like flowers in a vase. We had our Tennessee limit of stripers, and I was hooked on the fun for life.

Sonar expertise plays a huge part in striper fishing success. This species roams the lake almost constantly, and documented studies have shown certain fish sporting little radio transmitters traveled over 20 miles up or down a lake in only a matter of days! On the other hand, I have found stripers on or near the same structure for many days in succession. It may have been a seasonal change in their travel plans, or maybe the structure was so appealing that a new school moved in every time an old one left. I can't say which.

Stripers are very structure-oriented just like other game fish, even though they often cruise the big, open-water areas in a lake. Here the fish probably are following the old river

*Trolling for stripers in early March is a productive way
to get tired muscles.*

Credit: Tennessee Wildlife Resources Agency

Topwater action with stripers can be fantastic fun.

channel, despite the fact it may be 50 or 100 feet below.

Stripers also have a habit of intimidating schools of shad, literally ''herding'' them into a cove or pocket somewhere, then chopping them up viciously on a feeding spree. At these times, structure may not enter the picture in relation to what is *beneath* the fish, but water depth and the ability to confine their prey becomes important. When stripers chase baitfish into a shallow part of the lake to feed, you can see the surface action from quite a distance. And when you find yourself in the middle of a feeding school like that, it sounds as if someone is throwing concrete blocks into the water. The first time you experience this, you may fear for the safety of·small children in the boat.

You can tie on almost any old lure you like and feed it to the fish, as long as the action stays frantic. Topwater enthusiasts go absolutely bananas over this sort of thing.

Finding a ravenous school of stripers reducing the shad population in shallow water is indeed fun. But it happens only rarely to the fisherman who has to work for a living. The great majority of your fish probably will be taken from April to September by using live bait techniques. You find the school with your sonar, position the boat over them with the trolling motor, and fish straight down. In warm weather the fish may be cruising at about 15 to 20 feet below the surface. In hot weather they often go much deeper. I have caught them at depths of 50 feet.

Where legal, live bream are very popular for spring and summer striper fishing bait. Shiners and goldfish work well, too. And below many dams, you can employ a long-handle net to scoop shad for bait, as they often swim in huge schools along the bank when the utility people are generating power. If a striper is even slightly hungry, he will smack a shad presented to his nose. Bream are probably the next best choice for bait.

The trick is to use your depthfinder in locating the stripers, then place your bait at exactly the depth where they are, keeping it there with the help of a lead sinker a foot or two above the hook. If the fish signals from the school are showing up at 20 feet on your unit, you want that bait to be exactly 20 feet under the transducer. Many live-bait striper fishermen wrap colored thread around their fishing rods a measured 12 inches from the face of their reel. Using the 12-inch mark on the rod, they strip out line with their hand, counting the feet until the desired depth for the bait has been reached. It works beautifully!

If you have a good depthfinder, and if there is very little wind or current to pull your line to the side, you can *watch* your bait go down through the cone of the transducer. You don't have to count out the distance for accuracy; just let the bait fall in the water as you watch it on the depthfinder. When it reaches the fish, you can see it has arrived and engage the reel. Obviously, if you do not drop your bait down through the path of the transducer cone, you can't watch it fall.

Live bait fishing becomes something of a chore if the fish are not hungry. You can stay on top of them half the day and never get a strike. Fortunately, those situations are somewhat rare. Even if the school is not taking offers, there usually are a few mean and aggressive characters down there who will whack your bait just for the pure hell of killing it.

Live bait fishing also offers you your best shot at taking stripers on ultra-light tackle. The idea may sound a bit incredulous in light of how these fish behave when hooked, but if your depthfinder shows no trees or other brush below when stripers are found, you might pull it off. I must confess that catching stripers on ultra-light tackle is a passion of mine. Few things match the thrill and challenge.

If you really want to test your skills with rod and reel, spool up some light line on a small outfit and take a crack at getting a striper in the boat with it. You must be sure there are no underwater structures nearby that can cause problems for the light line. Examine the bottom carefully with your depthfinder, increasing the sensitivity a bit. Placing a sharp hook into a striper's mouth seems to give him an almost uncontrollable urge to tie monofilament knots around tree branches.

Vertical jigging for stripers can produce excellent tablefare, also. Almost any of the rectangular metal jigs or

*When the depthfinder shows an absence of underwater
trees, you can take a crack at catching
stripers on ultra-light.*

lead spoons will work quite well, providing they have sufficient weight to be worked effectively. A chunk of pork rind sometimes gives the lure more appeal. Other lures, like lead-heads with plastic tails, will produce, also. In fact, I caught a World Record striper vertical jigging with a lure like that.

My fishing pal Jack Ray and I were fishing in Norris Lake during October. We found a few stripers holding quite deep, and began trying to entice them with a five-inch Sassy Shad. The lure is heavy, has a soft, flexible tail, and is well-suited to the effort. The action was not very spectacular until we decided to leave.

The fish Jack had spotted on his sonar were right near the bottom in 52-foot water. After only limited success at this particular location, Jack was ready to move and suggested we reel up our lines. I took a couple of cranks on my reel and the line stopped coming up. It began going out.

Norris Lake is clear and deep. An old lake in the TVA chain, its trees and stump rows have long since gone the way of the dinosaurs, leaving the lake bottom clean and snag-free. Jack is also an ultra-light fan when it comes to stripers, and we were taking advantage of the lake conditions. I believe Jack was using either four or six-pound line. I was using eight-pound stuff on a spanking new rod and reel fresh from the box.

When the fish took my departing jig, I set the hook and the fun began. More accurately, the waiting began. It's hard to get a striper's full attention when you can't exert a great deal of pressure because of light line. Granted, eight-pound line is barely considered to be in the ultra-light family, but this was a case where my initial concern was finding out the prowess of my new equipment. I saw no reason to break off fish with the lighter line while learning how far I could push the stress factor on the new gear.

Anyhow, after the fish had taken us on a tour of the lower end of the lake, he tired of the game and began to fight. Jack and I both knew from the way he acted that this was a good fish. He was heavy, and he stayed well down in the water. After much sweat in the October crispness, I got the striper to the surface, where he rolled like a walrus in a feather bed.

We eased the boat over to the fish carefully as I kept the rod high and the line tight. (One does not drag a big fish across the water to one's boat when one is using light line, unless one wishes to hear one's line say "ping.") The fish was boated, and his length exceeded the width of Jack's big bass boat. He lay there with his nose jammed against the rod compartment on one side of the boat and his tail curled up the gunwale on the other. Nice fish.

The fish weighed 35-pounds 1-ounce after Jack insisted I remove my thumb from the scales. It was a definite World Record for freshwater stripers on eight-pound line. I documented the whole deal and mailed the official application along with the required line sample and the whole works. Unfortunately, my fish picked the incorrect time in history to get caught.

Two or three outfits were keeping freshwater fishing records at the time. When I caught my trophy, a larger striper on eight-pound line had not been documented anywhere. Then they all merged together. The IGFA in Ft. Lauderdale was the surviving custodian of World Records, and my record application was finally bounced their way. They acknowledged receipt and authenticity, and during the entire time they were consolidating records, no one documented a better striper in my Line Class.

Unfortunately, IGFA said they do not recognize feats

Author displays World Record striper for eight-pound line. Author also is only one who recognizes that record.

of skill with stripers on six-pound line, although they keep tally for catches on larger and on smaller line weights. Years earlier a bigger fish than mine had been captured on six-pound line, and that catch was therefore placed into the next higher line category. Yep. You got it. I am probably the only person in recorded history who caught, officially documented and *still holds* a World Record but never got the recognition. I have two words which I use to describe this lousy turn of events. One is "bull."

Topwater excitement, striper style, can lead to coronary problems. Usually during the first six weeks of spring's warming weather, stripers are prone to explode the water beneath a jumbo-size lure swimming across the surface. Good equipment and good fishing techniques are essential. Nerves of steel are recommended.

In contrast to the occasional times when feeding stripers can be seen ripping shad and splashing water from great distances, most topwater excitement will come when the action is far less visable. You may see no indication whatever of stripers in the area. The surface may be calm and unbroken. Sometimes there will be a swirl or two which betrays their presence.

Stripers will rocket up through ten or more feet of water to nail a topwater lure. I have found them ready and anxious to do this on many mornings, and sometimes even all day long if the skies are overcast. When fish are holding near the bottom close to islands, underwater humps and bends in the channel, they cannot always be spotted with your depthfinder without spooking them. Once they get on down there, say 15 feet or more, the boat doesn't seem to

*When stripers blast jumbo topwater lures, the
excitement builds dramatically.*

bother them quite as much (unless you rev the engine).

A thing like topwater action with stripers is not a matter usually kept secret by profit-conscious dock operators. Many (not all) of them will point you to within a few hundred yards of where the reported action is happening. If you can get that close, reasonable use of sonar will surely allow you to find the shelf, hump or bend they are using that morning. Look for it in water under 15 feet deep. Long, sloping points can be the ideal spot for searching.

When you find a likely-looking chunk of flooded real estate, very quietly back away to about the maximum distance you can cast a big lure. The magnum Redfins and Rebel topwater jobs are generally accepted as best for this. Chunk it as far over or across the flat as you can, then let it sit a second or two. It's a good idea to remove slack from your line the instant the lure splashes down. Many times, that's when the fish pops it. The retrieve with these six to nine-inch lures should be painfully slow. All you want to do is force the lure to make a ''V'' wake on the surface as it comes back in. No jerks, no trying to make it pop and gurgle, and no darting, stop-start action. Just a slow, deliberate retrieve across the surface. It drives 'em wild!

Perhaps this is too obvious to mention, but topwater striper fishing requires pretty strong line. I don't suggest you take a crack at it with mono that tests under 12 pounds. And 15-pound stuff is probably better. Some of the boat-for-hire cowboys in these parts use 30-pound line, maybe bigger. However, I think using anything over 20-pound test will restrict the distance you can cast the lure.

For reasons best known by the fish, stripers very often strike violently at a topwater plug but miss it by as much as a foot. When you have made a long cast, allowed the plug to rest momentarily, and then begun the slow retrieve, you

Credit: Tennessee Wildlife Resources Agency

Setting the hook on a striper that hits a surface plug should be almost a matter of self-defense.

logically hope something will happen. Your nervous system is coiled like a compressed steel spring, your heart is beating excitedly and your eyes and ears are straining for any evidence of a strike. When it happens, you react instantly. Without practice, you can't do otherwise. I've seen big husky men snatch a Redfin 65 feet through the air to the boat after a striper erupted two feet behind the lure. I can't say how far the lure actually traveled in the air. I was too busy ducking the treble hooks as it sailed by my head and continued on.

The trick is to convince your nerves that awesome explosion in the water by your lure really is nothing to worry about. Quaaludes and self-hypnosis are two ways of doing this. But done properly, the act of setting the hook should come almost in self-defense. When the monster smashes your lure, you *feel* it. When he misses it, you don't. You may water your trouser leg, but you don't feel the fish on the line. Set the hook only when you feel the hit.

When a striper misses a topwater plug, you should calmly stop the forward motion of the lure and let it sit there motionless. I use the word "calmly" in jest. But you *should* stop the lure. After perhaps four or five seconds, begin the slow retrieve again. Often, the fish will attack it a second time. I have had up to *five* separate strikes on a single cast, the final one coming as I lifted the bait from the water. Wouldn't you know, *that* was the time the fish decided he wanted to eat instead of play! My rod broke in three places as he wrapped it over the gunnel and under the boat in the blink of an eye. He looked to be about a 30-pounder.

On the days when cloud cover remains overhead for an extended time, you can catch topwater stripers practically the entire time if you can stay with them. Occasionally, a heavy morning or afternoon overcast will make the fish

Jack Ray grins over two-day limit of stripers. Finding the fish with sonar is the key.

come up even in summer, especially if the cloudy situation comes after a fresh, soft rain.

Live bait fishing, vertical jigging, trolling or casting topwater, stripers will give you a thrill a minute if not more. They offer some heavy-duty brawls for the angler who can find them on the lake. And you can do it regularly with what you know about sonar.

Fun Fish

Panfish are the most plentiful, most cooperative and probably the most overlooked fish in the country. You'll find them thriving in every ZIP Code from Seattle to Miami, and little short of a Grade IV Cataclysm can reduce their numbers substantially. Rabbits could take multiplication lessons from panfish.

It has been said you could pull up a fence post, fill the hole with water, and return a week later to find five bluegill swimming there. I doubt this is true. Two bluegill maybe, but not five.

Having earned a ''living'' as an outdoor writer for the past several years, it is only natural that I have accumulated a reasonable amount of fishing tackle in the process. After all, the career pursuit allows me to spend seven or eight days each week fishing with rod and reel, camera and typewriter. The fact our garage is jammed from floor to ceiling with this reasonable collection of tackle makes it necessary to park the family car outside in the weather.

By hard-won mutual consent, the estimated cost for all this equipment is never mentioned during conversations with my spouse. I have always considered these items to be necessary tools in the furtherance of my profession.

Most youngsters begin their fishing careers with
panfish. With a depthfinder in your boat,
you can increase the fun.

Her definition was less logical.

There is one variety of fishing that doesn't require 76 pounds of tackle to enjoy. When you go to the lake or creek to try your hand at catching panfish, you can carry your gear to the boat without working up a sweat. Carrying your catch back to the car can be where the work begins.

I never lost my love as a boy for the simple and predictable success offered by panfish. Webster defines "panfish" smugly as any fish that will fit into a pan. As a kid, I never really cared about the size and shape of the fish I caught, and species identification was pretty low on the list of importance, too. Small bass, bream (sunfish), crappie, catfish, etc.; they all were fun to catch on a cane pole.

Today I continue to enjoy the fun with panfish, but

have learned a few things which make it even easier to do. There is no doubt you can stand on the bank almost anywhere, and with a fat worm and a little patience, catch panfish. However, if you care to increase the fun, you should try this adventure from a boat, using your depthfinder to locate the better action.

Like most species, panfish are structure-oriented. They are found in creeks, farm ponds, large reservoirs and everything in between with the possible exception of a few rain barrels in Cleveland. "Structure" can be almost anything which alters the bottom of the lake or the shoreline. Treetops, stumps, weed beds, points and drop-offs are all examples of certified, fish-holding structure. As such, you can paddle or motor to these places, use your sonar to pinpoint the structure, and set up shop for the fun.

Crappie love to associate with wooden structure, especially during spring months. You'll find them hanging out around boat docks, piers, brush piles, stumps, etc. Later during the hot months, crappie live along the many drop-offs further out in the lake where the bottom depth changes quickly around the old river channel.

Bream, "brim," and sunfish simply love the water! You'll find them conducting business practically anywhere it's wet. They do enjoy living along the shoreline, primarily, but the larger ones most often are found out in slightly deeper water. They also prefer structure which offers them a hiding place in case of emergencies and a bit of shade for bright summer days. Bream often frequent the popular spots for crappie, including the deep-water drop-offs, although these more open areas sometimes make them nervous because of larger predators in the vicinity.

Catfish move around more in the lake, but they normally come up in depth during the late afternoon hours,

Finding the proper habitat with sonar can put nice cats like this one into your net.

feeding across more shallow points or underwater islands. Drop-offs and rocky points are favorite haunts for catfish. The channel catfish has a preference for moving water when available. They are much more likely to be found out on the ends of points or near the river channel, instead of well back into the slack water in coves.

Bass, including the white bass, are often found around points extending out from the bank. Structure seems to be more important to largemouth bass than either smallmouth or white bass; the last two species often contented to suspend in the water near structure instead of hiding under it.

As you can see, in a great many instances the home base for these species of fish often overlaps. That's one of the neat things about catching panfish. You don't have to look for a magic "honey hole" that requires elaborate searching with sonar. To catch panfish, all you have to do is go somewhere in the ball park, and one or more of the species should be present.

Equipment needs are simple just like the process of finding the fish. Mark Twain's boys used a willow branch, sewing thread and a single hook. Worms and grasshoppers did the rest. The same outfit will work today, although most people seem to prefer monofilament line instead of sewing thread.

Successful days with panfish require far less complicated gear than is required for the pursuit of most other species. Cane poles are tough to beat. An ultra-light outfit can add both versatility and increased fun to your efforts. And a fly rod can do double duty, serving as a substitute cane pole for live bait and/or performing its intended role in life casting flies.

The main idea is to keep your tackle small in size. Four or six-pound line is helpful in casting tiny jigs. Slightly

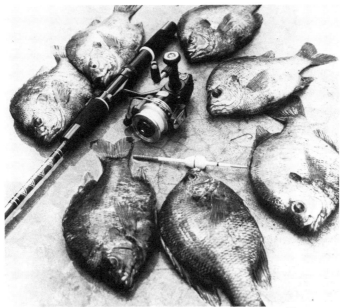

Small jigs worked slowly in productive areas will usually result in a mixed bag of panfish.

heavier line is O.K. when the water is cloudy. Hook size remains small, except when working deeper drop-offs where larger fish may be caught accidentally-on-purpose. If you use a float or bobber, use one that barely supports your bait. Don't use one of those huge round things that would float a brick. The fish can feel resistance when he tugs on one of those.

Jigs are deadly on all panfish if you keep them on the miniature side. They can be cast out and retrieved slowly, or they can be positioned beneath a small float. Use the very smallest jig you can control with your rod and reel. Even the

When the willow flies hatch, all panfish
gorge themselves.

tiny $\frac{1}{32}$-ounce jobs are not too small to produce fine action. Light line and a tailwind makes it possible to cast them.

Very small spoons and spinners account for sundry truckloads of panfish annually. During summer months you'll find super action with small popping bugs on a fly rod, courtesy of hungry bream early and late in the day. In spring and fall, they will attack a sinking fly vigorously. And of course, when the willow flies hatch out, all panfish gorge themselves. Bream, crappie and catfish will chomp practically any type fly you wish to flip into the fracus.

Another big bonus which makes catching panfish easy comes from their menu of jointly-consumed baits and lures. All of the species will take worms, crickets, minnows, jigs and spinners. You don't have to change bait or technique

every time you find a different species around the bend.
Panfish have overlapping habitat and similar taste buds.

I'll be the first to admit that dunking worms along the
shoreline is a fine way to catch bream, and that standing on
the bank jiggling a live minnow in a treetop will catch
plenty of crappie in the spring. You don't have to use
depthfinders for either activity. But if you want to increase
the fun materially, back your boat offshore a bit and try
using a small jig with a *small* minnow attached to it. You'll
catch bream, bass, crappie and catfish!

Even without a minnow attached, a small jig placed
below a tiny float can be a fantastic tool for boating panfish
in great numbers. Cast and retrieve slowly. Very slowly. Or
just let the wind and wave action put a little action into the
suspended jig while the float sits there. Sometimes, no
movement at all works best. The float will keep your jig at
the desired depth and just out of the reach from snags and
aggressive underwater tree limbs. It's an extremely effective method for taking panfish. While one jig is resting
under the float, another small cousin can be crawled or
gently "hopped" across the bottom with a second rod and
reel to capture good numbers of catfish in the very same
area.

The double-hook crappie rig described earlier is a killer
on panfish when worked around structure and drop-offs. A
pair of minnows on this rig worked carefully up and down
the drop-offs in a lake or river can catch a real variety of
tablefare. This is especially true in hot weather fishing.

Panfish are affected by water temperatures and oxygen
levels like all other fish. Sometimes they are forced to suspend themselves between the bad water on bottom and the
hot water on top. This comfort zone is called the thermocline. When this happens, your depthfinder can pick them

Credit: Lowrance Electronics, Inc.

When oxygen becomes a problem in the lake, you can
spot the situation easily with your graph. There simply
won't be any fish life in the bad water.

out with routine efficiency. Even if the fish happen to be
suspended inside the treetop, turning down your sonar sensitivity reveals their presence there.

Suspended fish are harder to catch because you must
offer your bait at the correct level. Bouncing a lure on the
bottom won't catch fish if there is no oxygen down there.
There won't be any fish down there, either. The sonar tells
you at what depth the fish are holding, and you pattern your
presentation around that statistic. This, too, is a great time
to use a small float above a jig.

Concentrate your searching for panfish into two general areas. There is no point running the boat all over the
lake while wasting gasoline and time. Work the shoreline
structure first, then move out further to check out the drop-

Credit: Tennessee Wildlife Resources Agency

*Depthfinder use opens the door to increased fun with
all species, year-around.*

offs. In most lakes, you can catch all the panfish you care to
clean in an area covering less than a half-mile square. You
will find panfish all year around on either the shoreline
structure or the deeper drops. You may not find all species
of panfish crowding around the exact same piece of structure, and you won't get a strike every time you drop over a
hook. But you *can* find several species on the same structure, and you *can* catch panfish practically every time out.

If you really want to stack the odds in your favor, put a
can of worms, a bucket of minnows and a handful of small
jigs in the boat. Work only the two basic types of structure
suggested. By process of elimination, you can find the combination of bait, structure and depth that produces action.
You'll find this rarely fails, even on days when everyone
else returns to the dock empty-handed.

6

Graph Paper Interpretation

More on Reading Graphs

On these pages you will find several examples of chart paper which illustrate points previously covered in the text. Most were burned with the unit set on the 60-foot scale, and each example should provide an opportunity for you to polish your reading and interpretation skills. (Try to figure out the main characters on the paper *before* reading the caption!) The examples apply to video images, also.

There will be obvious differences in the way images appear on graphs from various manufacturers. To my knowledge, no two manufacturers have graphs on the market which print or burn signals exactly alike. Don't let this bother you. Look for patterns, groupings and consistent display of detail when comparing these examples to those you have run with your own unit.

I chose to use graph paper examples from only one brand unit, with few exceptions. This is not an indication of favoritism. Had I done otherwise, the lack of similarity between graph paper printout could have been confusing.

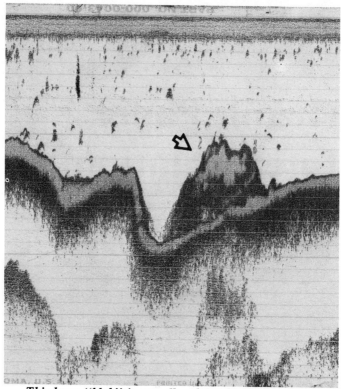

This huge "blob" is actually a large brushpile put out in the lake by crappie fishermen to attract fish. Excess use of the grayline control causes it to shade out in the center, making interpretation difficult.

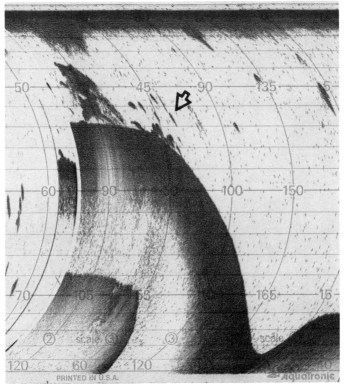

Curve-line graphs are a bit tough to interpret until you have worked with them adequately. This is an excellent picture of active bass working on the structure where they have made physical contact. The larger images are from a school of shad that may be in serious trouble in a few minutes!

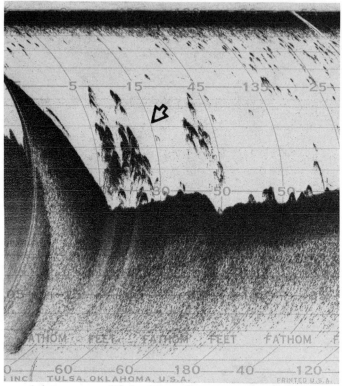

*A large mass of fish with medium separation indicates
school of either crappie or white bass. Because of the
Christmas tree formation, these are probably white
bass. If in doubt, drop a small jig into the
school and find out!*

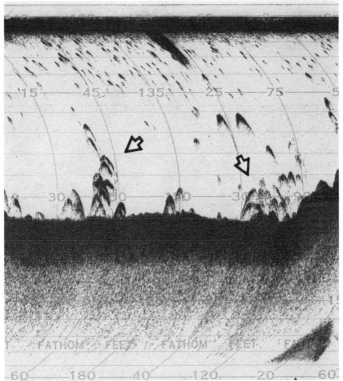

*Here's proof! Both these groups of fish are holding
inside a treetop. With the sensitivity turned down until
the tree itself fades away, the fish
echoes remain strong.*

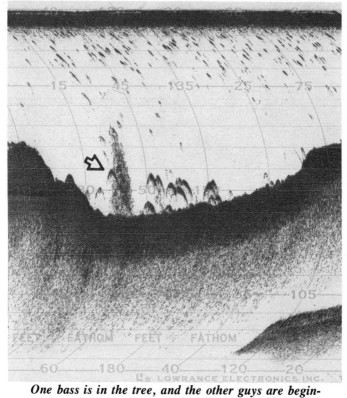

*One bass is in the tree, and the other guys are begin-
ning to school more tightly together. Get ready, these
fish are about to have supper!*

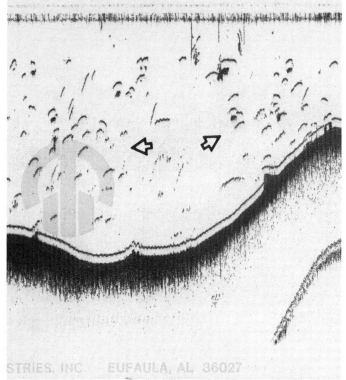

Fish on the left are very loosely schooled over a large area. Group on the right has begun to school a bit more tightly, and appear to be moving to contact the structure. When they touch it, or get up on top, they will be highly catchable.

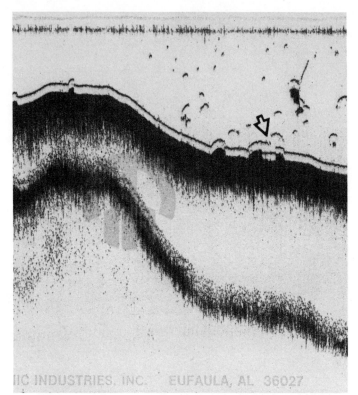

When you do not use the suppressor control, some of the better graph units can display fish holding almost right on the bottom without blending the signals. That fish is practically scratching his tummy on a stump!

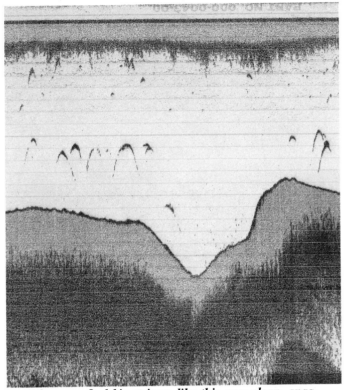

When you find big stripers like this over clean, snag-free bottom, it's time to break out the ultra-light tackle!

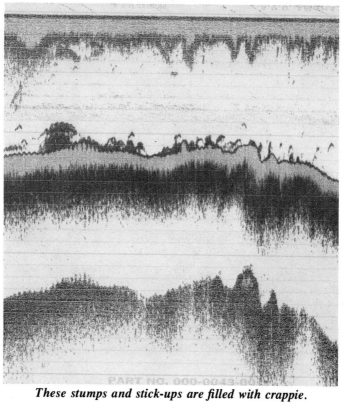

These stumps and stick-ups are filled with crappie.

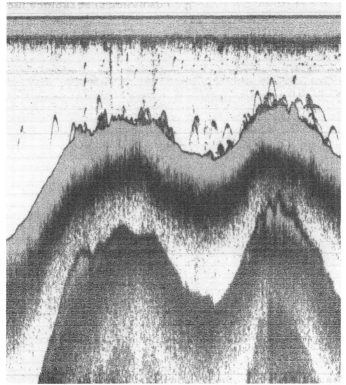

*A genuine fisherman's delight! Both of these ridges are
filled with large, active fish.*

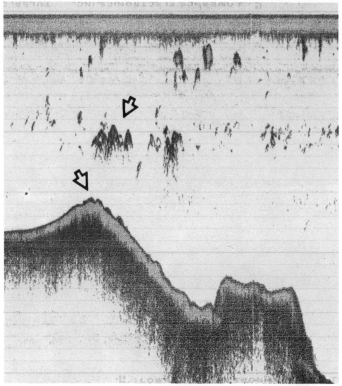

Bass suspend at whatever depth is comfortable for them when the lake has an oxygen problem. You can tell when they are active because they will move into position directly over the structure when they begin to feed. This school is relating to that underwater hump, and you can see they have taken position properly to indicate they are feeding. Vertical jigging in that school produced excellent results!

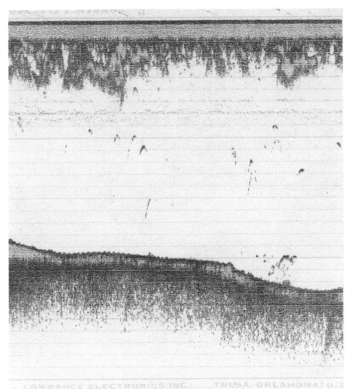

A huge school of white bass just beneath the surface.
Shad would be more tightly packed together, displaying
a solid mass on the paper.

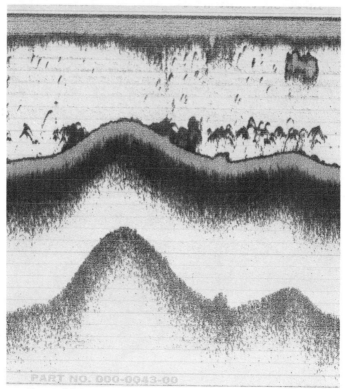

It would be pretty hard to find better action than this chart paper reveals. Good sized fish are packed in there on both sides of the ridge. Notice how they all seem to prefer the same depth water.

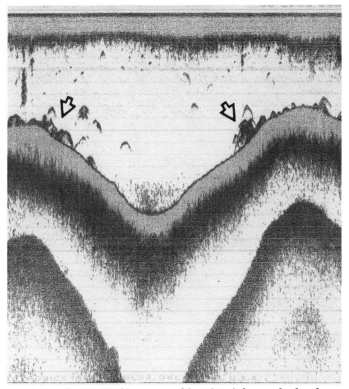

Active bass attacking everything in sight on both of these drop-offs. Fish signals are mixed in with those of stumps and brush, indicating there is no doubt they have made physical contact with the structure and are feeding.

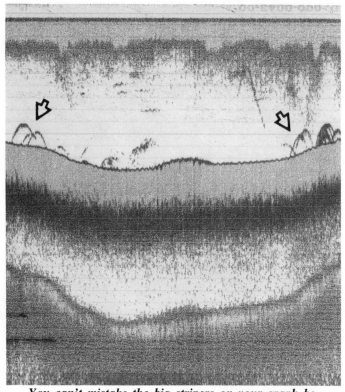

You can't mistake the big stripers on your graph because of their size. These are on bottom at about 25 feet.

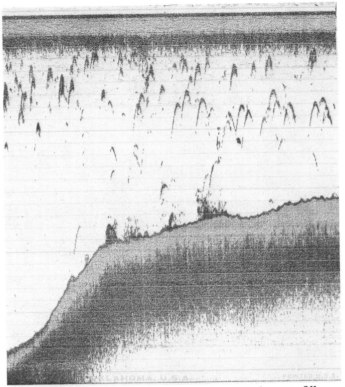

Trolling for stripers in March/April is a good way to fill your freezer. These stripers are holding at about 17 feet.

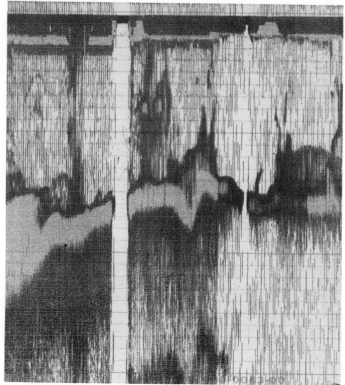

For Pete's sake, Charlie; turn that other unit OFF!

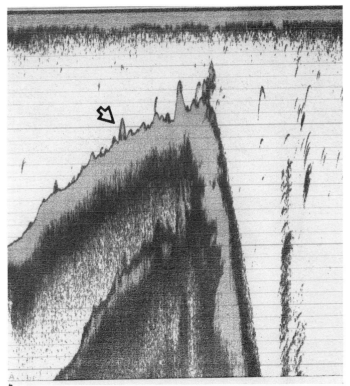

Excessive use of the suppressor control will "blend" signals together. This graph shows fish holding tightly on the bottom, but the suppressor control is set too strong, making the fish signals merge into the bottom signals.

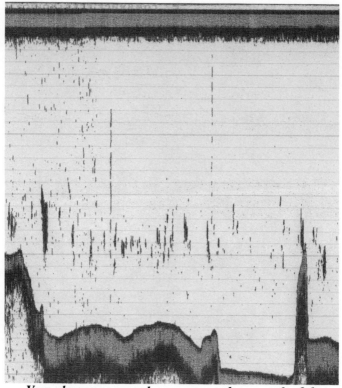

*Very slow paper speed on your graph can make fish
signals appear as straight vertical lines.*

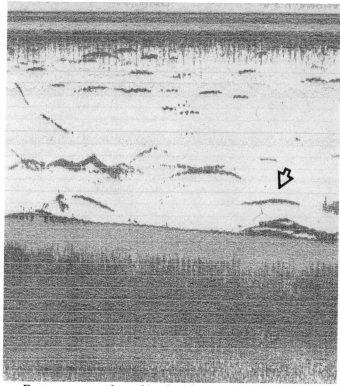

*Fast paper speed combined with very slow boat speed
can cause fish signals to be drawn as
long horizontal lines.*

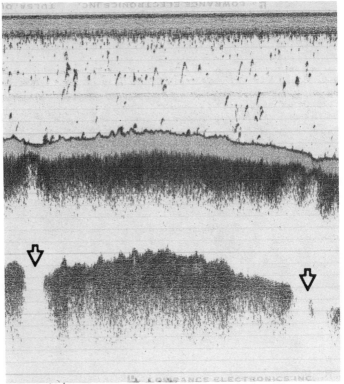

*Even minor changes in bottom composition will cause
the grayline feature to narrow on the paper, and the
second bottom echo will disappear.*

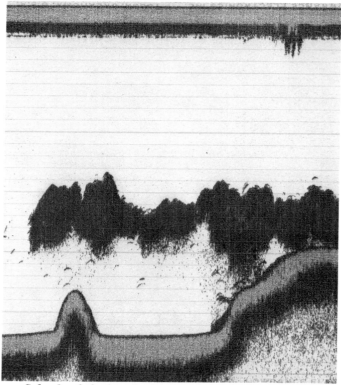

*Schools of shad pack closely together, appearing as a
single large ''blob'' on both flashers and graphs.*

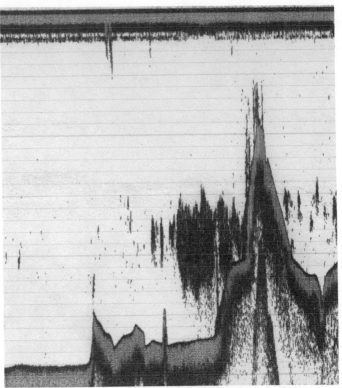

*It's almost impossible to get meaningful details on a
depthfinder if the boat speed exceeds 30 mph.*

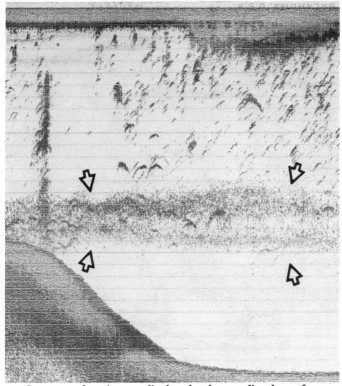

Some graph units can display the thermocline layer for you due to the sudden change of water density when the temperature drops. Note the absence of fish life below the thermocline in this lake.

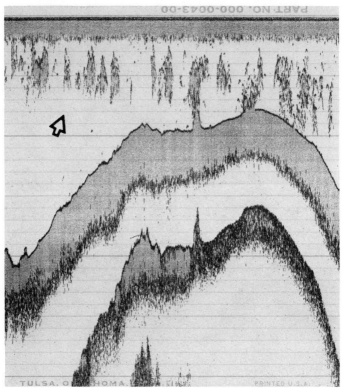

Schools of white bass like this can sometimes cover several acres in size. Note vague resemblance to Christmas trees in shape of formations.

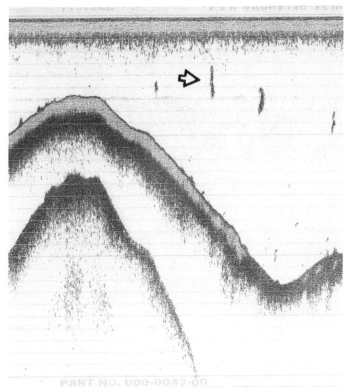

Vertical stacked arches out in open space.
Probably air bubbles.

7

Winding Up Business

Maintenance Requirements for Sonar

Even the very finest depthfinders on the market today are subject to failure sometime. You can cause the failure to come about prematurely by not taking a few common sense precautions, and by not taking care of the unit properly.

Like any sophisticated piece of circuitry, depthfinders can experience mechanical problems from wear, abuse or perhaps a simple construction defect which slipped past the Quality Control people at the plant. Regardless of how the problem occurs, the only time you will discover the fault is while on the water. And that is, of course, the exact time when you need the unit to work! Lost fishing time while the depthfinder goes to the shop is certainly a problem. The repair bill after the warranty expires can be quite another source of frustration. There is little advantage to be gained by being careless in the area of depthfinder maintenance.

The following suggestions for delaying or avoiding mechanical problems are worth heeding.

The Owner's Manual which accompanies your sonar machine home from the store should have some pertinent info on the subject of maintenance for your particular unit. *Read the manual* and follow the manufacturer's advice! Below are some tips which may, or may not, appear in that manual.

Transducers. Your transducer is the "eye" for your whole sonar system. If it gets in trouble, nothing else works efficiently. The transducer contains a crystal which must be protected from sharp blows. If your location for the transducer was at the rear of the boat on the outside of the transom, you should give special consideration to the potential problems of high-speed boat travel where the possibility of striking a floating object exists.

Transom-mounted transducers also are exposed to oil and gas residue floating on the water in a busy marina. If you keep your boat in a slip at the marina, the problem potential compounds materially. Oil which is allowed to remain on the face of a transducer can coat the eye, decreasing performance of your system. In time, oil can totally blind the transducer, making it necessary to purchase another one. Road film picked up while trailering the boat to and from the lake can coat the transducer, as can algae build-up in the water when it remains idle for long periods.

It is essential that you clean the transducer face frequently if it is exposed to these hazards. Use a wash rag dipped in warm soapy water to scrub the transducer face several times each season.

Transducers mounted inside the boat to shoot signals through the hull require less attention. However, a poor mounting job, or a sharp rap on the hull beneath the trans-

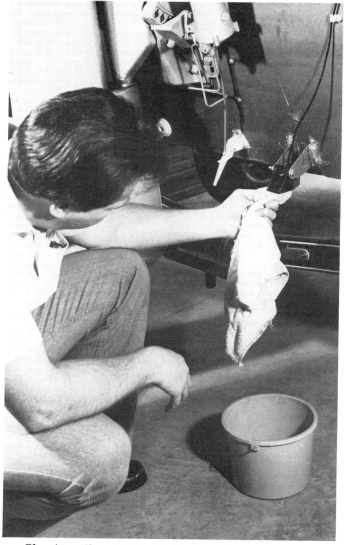

Cleaning oil and dirt off the face of your transom-mounted transducer is essential to optimum readout.

ducer, can cause a crack to appear under the puck. Examine the mount regularly for signs of separation, as oil will seep under the surface at the first opportunity. If you used silicone to mount your transducer, it may be eaten away rather quickly by petroleum products, so frequent inspections are mandatory. And even with the transducer attached securely to the hull with epoxy, cleaning out the sump area annually can protect the transducer cord from harsh chemicals. And it doesn't hurt anything to drop a bar of Ivory soap into the sump and leave it there, either.

Electrical Connections. Maintenance of your battery connections, and all other electrical connections affecting your depthfinders, is keenly important. Actually, it's critical. If your unit is of the portable variety with self-contained

batteries, remove them when the equipment is not in use to eliminate the chance of leakage and/or corrosion. Where the depthfinder is mounted permanently in the boat, eyeball the battery connections *constantly* to spot early stages of corrosion. It's a fine idea to make yourself develop the habit of checking the battery connections every time you fill the gas tank in the boat during the boating season, and then go to the garage to check same every two or three weeks during the off-season while the boat sits idle.

Remove and clean all connections as frequently as needed. Minor corrosion build-up problems can be removed efficiently with 400-grit sandpaper and a dedication for being thorough. Remove all traces of the problem-causing corrosion from battery terminal posts and wires which are to

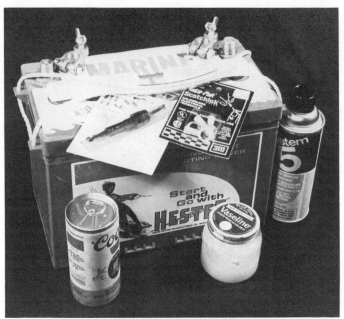

*Keep your battery terminals sparkling clean. Coat the
posts and connections with grease
or Vaseline after cleaning.*

be attached. When the battery terminals and connectors are
genuinely clean and corrosion free, coat them heavily with
grease or Vaseline. Reclean and regrease the terminals
every two or three months, especially in hot weather.

All this may sound like a bit too much attention to give
battery connections. It is not; I promise you. A chap named
Pat McCann, who is a master mechanic in the sonar world
and who operates one of the nation's largest depthfinder
repair centers, emphasizes the fact. According to McCann,
a surprising number of units sent in for repair came as a

Credit: Lowrance Electronics, Inc.

result of fishermen not taking the time to clean and maintain their battery terminals!

McCann says when battery terminals are allowed to corrode and oxidize, they will "float" electrically. Even when the connectors are clamped on very tightly, they can become disconnected electrically. Then when the big engine on your boat fires up initially and turns a few high rpm, it can apply excessive volt "spikes" which then bypass the battery because of the corrosion, and enter the circuitry of your depthfinder. This surge destroys transistors and circuits, making a trip to the Repair Center necessary. (Your depthfinder is not the only item in the boat which can be injured under these circumstances. CB radios, solid state

The King 1350 straight line graph has computer selected pulse length with manual override.

ignitions and tachometers are also vulnerable.)

Corrosion can invade the unit's power plug, transducer jack, fuse holder or power cord splices, too. And this creates poor readings for you at best, unit failure at worse. Check and clean these potential trouble spots frequently.

The smooth shaft of your transducer plug-in is easy enough to clean with fine sandpaper, but when gunk forms inside the power plug, it can cause headaches. Some power plugs can be disassembled for cleaning. Most cannot. You end up wearing off the skin on your thumb and forefinger trying to twirl a rolled-up piece of sandpaper within the small confines of the plug interior.

Your best bet for reducing corrosion inside the power plug comes from not letting it happen in the first place. If you put the plug inside a small plastic bag, secured by a rubber band or little wire tie strip, it will not suffer build-up

*A small plastic sack can be used to protect the power
plug and transducer jack from corrosion
when not in use.*

when not in use. The bag offers protection, even if your
boat must be left outside in the weather. A shot into the plug
with WD-40 or LPS2 will help also.

Special Procedures for Graphs. Graph units generate
dust (carbon) inside the case as they burn images on the
paper. This dust should be removed regularly. Holding the
unit over your head and blowing into it will do little more
than transfer a good bit of the dust from the unit into your
eyes and hair. A better procedure would be with the aid of a
low-pressure air hose. Blow out the dust with the pressure
hose, but be sure the compressed air is free from water
and/or oil. Hold the nozzle of the air hose far enough away
from the unit to protect the delicate wires and things inside.

After each half-dozen rolls of paper you run through

your graph, it is a good idea to moisten a clean cloth with alcohol and clean off the stylus belt and the wheels over which the belt runs. Do not use solvents which are stronger than the alcohol, and avoid abrasive cleaners for this job. The clear plastic viewing door of the graph and the metal or plastic plate behind the paper should be cleaned often with a soft rag dampened only with clean, fresh water.

Most graph recorders have a rubber roller which functions to draw or pull the paper through the unit. This roller will get covered with dust after long use and the build-up can make it slippery, causing the paper to move through the unit in an irregular manner. Clean the take-up roller with alcohol to eliminate the problem. A Q-tip or cotton swab works well for this task.

The stylus belt on many graphs will stretch with use. This creates poor image reproduction on the paper and/or gaps and blank spaces. When the stylus belt stretches, centrifugal force permits the stylus to move out and away from the paper, thus leaving no printout during the time it makes no contact. This usually occurs at readings between 20 and 30 feet on a 60-foot scale, or in the upper ⅓-area of the paper. Replace the stylus belt when this happens. If you're on the water when this becomes a problem, and you don't have a spare belt in the boat, try bending the stylus slightly more towards the paper. That should help until you can get another belt for replacement.

Miscellaneous Chores. It is important that you check the mounting bracket for your unit frequently. Even though you may have secured the bracket to the console with large bolts as suggested earlier, it can work loose after a while. Constant pounding and vibration do the dirty deed. When allowed to shake and rattle, your depthfinder experiences

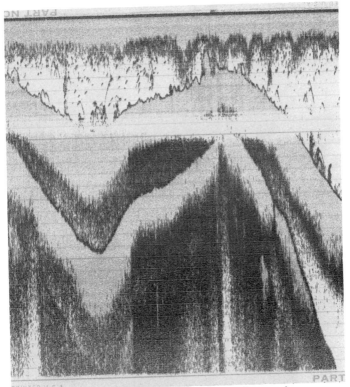

With use, some stylus belts will stretch, causing a blank space on the chart paper, usually in the upper ⅓-portion of the paper.

shorter life. Tighten down the mounting brackets to insure they remain secure at all times.

I suggest you remove your depthfinders from the boat while trailering to and from the lake. This eliminates unnecessary vibrations, and is an obvious deterrent to theft as well.

After use in salt water, your depthfinder should be

wiped off carefully. A cloth dampened with fresh water should do the trick completely. Just run the wet cloth over the exterior of the unit, not on the inside. And dunking the depthfinder in the bathtub to remove salt spray is not recommended at all!

Don't attempt to lubricate the moving parts of your depthfinder unless the Owner's Manual gives exact instruc-

A clear plastic bag can serve as a fine "raincoat" for your sonar unit on the lake.

tions on the process. Even then, use less lubricant than you think is needed, and keep your mitts away from the circuits.

Once or twice a season, check out the power and transducer cords in the boat for evidence of rubbing or chafing. Sometimes they wander from your original location, finding

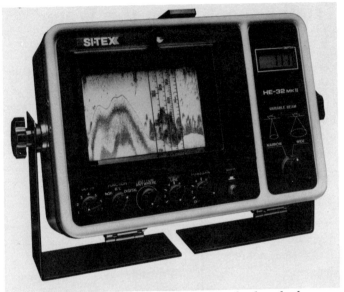

*SI-TEX HE-32 MK II Chart Recorder has dual
search, scale expansion, bottom lock and digital
display.*

sharp edges in the boat to make friends with. You may have
to tape these wires up and out of the way again.

Unless your depthfinder specifically states that it is
waterproof, it makes good sense to protect it from moisture
to the extent practical. Letting your depthfinder get totally
soaked in a downpour does little to improve sonar relations.
If the manufacturer provides a rain cover for the unit, use it.
A large plastic bag will perform the job of shedding water
for your unit, also. Protect your depthfinder just as you
would any other expensive piece of electronic gear. And if
the unit does become wet in a rainstorm, allow it to dry out
completely before putting it away in a confined storage area.

Troubleshooting on the Water

Any problem which causes your depthfinder not to work properly is a serious one. However, many of the solutions for those problems are relatively easy to perform, even while out on the lake. The following chart gives the three most common causes for sonar failure, and explains several things you can check out yourself before deciding the unit is due for a trip to the repairman.

Problem	Possible Solutions
Depthfinder is turned "ON" but nothing happens.	1—Check for blown fuse in the power cord. Replace. 2—Probable loose wire someplace. Check battery connections. Check power cord plug-in to unit. Possible dead battery. 3—Corrosion build-up on battery post or on power cord, connectors, etc. Clean and retighten connections.
Depthfinder produces a "0" reading, but does not show a bottom reading.	1—Check transducer plug-in to see if it is firmly inserted into the unit. Check for any corrosion build-up on plug. Clean plug if needed. 2—Transducer not making proper contact with the water. May have become ex-

	cessively coated with oil or dirt (transom mount). May have foreign object trapped over transducer face (transom mount). 3—Water exceeds maximum depth on scale being used and cannot be printed on paper (graphs). Switch to deeper depth scale. 4—Sensitivity control not turned up sufficiently to produce bottom reading. 5—Stylus on graph may be bent slightly. Adjust carefully by bending stylus gently toward paper with light finger pressure. 6—Transducer flopped in bracket, no longer pointing down correctly (transom mounts). Reposition transducer and tighten bracket.
Bottom readings and fish signals are faint, hard to read.	1—Transducer is dirty. Clean the face with a cloth or rub it vigorously with your fingers (transom mount). 2—Transducer needs time to become "wetted" after storage. Rub the face with your fingers to remove air bubbles (transom mount).

	3—Boat speed is too fast for getting detailed readings. If traveling under 30 mph, transducer angle on transom is probably incorrect. 4—Sensitivity setting probably is too low for water depth. Turn it up. 5—Stylus on graph wearing out or needs slight adjustment. Bend toward paper gently. Replace stylus if necessary. 6—Stylus belt may have stretched, causing poor readings on part of the graph paper. Replace belt if necessary. 7—Check viewing door on graph to see if dust accumulation inside has covered the clear window area. Clean door inside and outside with a soft cloth.

Finale

By its very nature, the subject of depthfinders is a very complex one. I have made an attempt to keep the contents of this book presented in a fashion which is easy to understand. This is in part due to my inability to write and understand the very technical stuff which electronic engineers talk about on coffee breaks. And in part because I think the

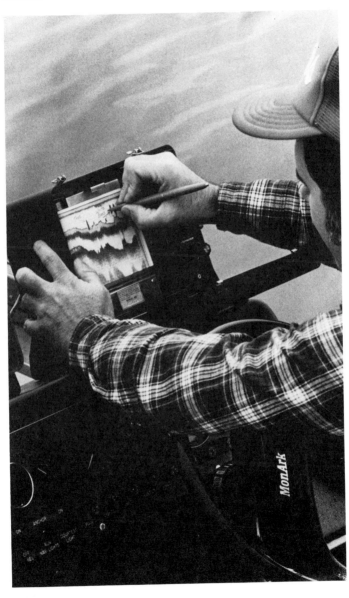

typical depthfinder owner really doesn't give a hoot about the statistics of circuitry which make the unit perform. He just wants to be able to use his sonar machine on the water to discover information which helps him put more fish in the bucket.

Hopefully, you have benefited from that approach.

When I selected the title for this book, I used the word "complete." This will require a few words on the use of depthfinders in salt water. Previously, it was mentioned that

Credit: Tennessee Wildlife Resources Agency

you should clean away the salt residue from the outside case of your unit immediately after returning home. There is another little problem involved should you use a transommounted transducer on an aluminum boat. The problem is called electrolysis.

Electrolysis occurs in both fresh and saltwater situations, but is much more common in the salt. Salt water is a better conductor for electrical current, which speeds the process substantially.

Many crappie fishing experts feel the larger crappie typically spawn in deeper water instead of along shore.

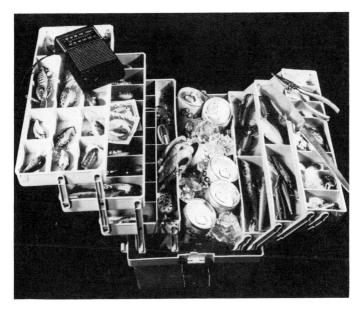

For saltwater use, do not purchase a bronze transducer to be used on an aluminum boat. Most manufacturers offer plastic transducers anyway. Use one. Electrolysis occurs where two dissimilar metals touch, particularly bronze and aluminum. The bronze seems to survive the encounter unscathed, but the aluminum will be eaten away. Plastic transducers foil the chemical reaction which causes electrolysis.

When bronze transducer cases are allowed to become grounded to the battery, as in the case of some older models and/or by accident, the results are alarmingly spectacular. On wood or fiberglass boats, current flow from the motor block to the transducer will eat up the transducer in *only a matter of hours,* and severe damage to the motor can result as an unwanted bonus.

Most boats and all major brand depthfinders have a

The Aqua Meter Cheater models use delayed receiver recovery and narrow pulse lengths to filter out extraneous flashes.

negative-ground system. If your boat has a positive-ground system, you *must* use a plastic transducer. It doesn't matter whether the rig is used in fresh water or salt. If in doubt, ask your marine dealer to check it out for you.

Differences in the way sound travels through salt water have little significance in the way your unit will perform if taken to the ocean on vacation. Slight, but not noticeable unless you measure your fun in inches at 100 yards. However, there is a material change in reading the very deep signals if you are using a typical high-frequency unit designed mainly for freshwater use.

High-frequency units in the 200 kHz range are designed to offer superior resolution between objects, but those high-frequency mechanics are absorbed more by particles in the water. Depthfinders specifically designed for use in salt water often have lower frequencies. These show the bottom accurately, and display *large* fish for you, but you can forget all the fancy footwork I described earlier about "fine points" in interpretation. Saltwater units with 1,000-foot depth scales sometimes have frequencies in the 50 kHz range. Those big boomers probably can shoot signals through the pollution in Biscayne Bay!

Recap and Conclusions

A few things bear repeating with a different choice of words. You have finished a compilation of facts and experiences which pretty well exhaust my knowledge on the subject of depthfinder usage. If you are to go forth with confidence and enjoy the benefits of sonar readout in your fishing success, there are a few things I would caution you to remember:

- There are many quality-conscious manufacturers of sonar equipment in America. There are many differences in unit capabilities, features and price tags which fill the dealers' shelves, too. I suggest you take time to make notes which describe your typical day afloat before going to the store in search of a sonar helper. Purchase the unit which offers you the best opportunity to get all information applicable to your personal fishing endeavors. During the selection process, you would be wise to consider the not-so-small matter of service and repair. Even the better units will fail sometimes, and ready service and repair facilities can become painfully important if your depthfinder decides to conk out exactly when the fishing action begins to boom. Price, features and service should be considered before plunking down your money for a new unit.

- Your transducer is the "weak link" in your entire sonar system. Failure to make proper installation or failure to maintain the transducer will result in lousy readout. Potential problems shooting a signal through the hull must be solved. The special problems which may come from using an aluminum boat with "thru the hull" readings are important to remember. The wise person will experiment with transducer location before mixing the epoxy. And there's the unnerving problem of electrolysis to consider, too.

- The controls, knobs, whistles and horns on your depthfinder all have a definite purpose, and it behooves you to understand each function completely. Special features on sonar units are not built in for cosmetic purposes. You should work with your depthfinder on the water as if it were an office employee who owed you money. The Owner's Manual gives you several basic points to consider, and these should be committed to memory. The remaining sonar skills you develop will come only with time and experience. Dedication to the learning process is the price you will pay for expertise.

- Personal prowess in signal interpretation results only from personal experience with your unit on the water. You cannot learn to interpret sonar information simply by reading a book on the subject. Even this one.

The depthfinder can become your most reliable tool for boosting the number of fillets you bring

home. It will not lie to you if properly installed
and operated. But you must be clever enough to
figure out what the unit is saying with its returning
signals, and then have the smarts to apply the
appropriate fishing techniques which pay off
under the circumstances spelled out by your unit.
You need sonar interpretation skills and a knowledge of fish habitat, seasonal patterns, etc.

- The proper care and maintenance of your sonar
system is essential to its health and long life. Lack
of attention to maintenance chores will surely result in decreased efficiency and eventual replacement of your depthfinders. Cleaning the battery
terminals, electrical connections and transom-
mounted transducer faces will be a regular re-
quirement for gaining full potential from your
sonar equipment over the years.

Proper maintenance of your electrical system cannot be
over-emphasized.

Appendix

This listing of depthfinder manufacturers/distributors was compiled thanks to information furnished by the American Fishing Tackle Manufacturers' Association, National Marine Manufacturers Association, SALT WATER SPORTSMAN Magazine and BOATING INDUSTRY Magazine.

ACR ELECTRONICS, Box 2148, Hollywood, FL 33020

AIRGUIDE INSTRUMENT CO., 2210 Wabansia Ave., Chicago, IL 60647

ANDREA RADIO CORP., 11-40 45th Rd., Long Island City, NY 11101

ANDREWS INSTRUMENTS, 8575 Mosley Rd., Houston, TX 77075

APELCO, 676 Island Pond Rd., Manchester, NH 03103

AQUA METER INSTRUMENT CORP., 465 Eagle Rock Ave., Roseland, NJ 07068

AQUASONIC ELECTRONICS, 13915 Denton Dr., Farmers Branch, TX 75234

ARNAV SYSTEMS, INC., 4740 Ridge Dr. NE 7078, Salem OR 97303

ATLANTIC MARINE, Box 508, Mechanicville, NY 12118

BAYMAR, 1705 Enterprise Dr., Fairfield, CA 94533

BH ELECTRONICS, 331 Bremer Bldg., St. Paul, MN 55101

BOATWORKS, INC., 71B Front St. Tuckers Wharf, Marblehead, MA 01945

BRISTOL ELECTRONICS, 651 Orchard St., New Bedford, MA 02744

BROOKES & GATEHOUSE, 154 E. Boston Post Rd.,
Mamaroneck, NY 10543

BYRD INDUSTRIES, Industrial Park, Ripley, TN 38063

CHANNEL MARINE, 424 Margate Rd., Ramsgate, Kent
CT 12 6SR ENGLAND

CHRIS BOCK INSTRUMENTS, 2313 Washington
Blvd., Marina del Rey, CA 90291

CMC COMMUNICATION, INC., 5479 Jetport Ind.
Blvd., Tampa, FL 33614

COAST NAVIGATION, 1934 Lincoln Dr., Annapolis,
MD 21401

COASTAL NAVIGATOR, 4925 Leary Way NW,
Seattle, WA 98107

COM MAR, INC., 70 West Main St., Northboro, MA
01532

COMMUNICATIONS ASSOC., 220 McKay Rd.,
Huntington Station, NY 11746

COMPASS ELECTRONICS CORP., 3700 24th Ave.,
Forest Grove, OR 97116

COPAL CORP OF AMERICA, 1600 Route 208,
Fairlawn, NJ 07410

DATAMARINE INT'L, 53 Portside Dr., Pocasset, MA
02559

DAVIS INSTRUMENTS, 642 143rd Ave., San Leandro,
CA 94578

W.H. DENOUDEN USA, INC., P.O. Box 8712,
Baltimore, MD 21240

EAGLE ELECTRONICS, P.O. Box 669, Catoosa, OK
74105

ELECTRO MARINE SYSTEMS, 96 Fox Hunt La., E.
Amherst, NY 14051

EPSCO MARINE, 411 Providence Hwy., Westwood, MA 02090

FISH DETECTION SYSTEMS, 21562 Newland St., Huntington Bch, CA 92649

FISH HAWK ELECTRONICS CORP, Box 340, Crystal Lake, IL 60014

FISHMASTER PRODUCTS, P.O. Box 9635, Tulsa, OK 74107

FLEET MARINE, 1820 N.E. 146th St., North Miami, FL 33181

FURUNO USA, 271 Harbor Way, S. San Francisco, CA 94080

GEMTRONICS (GEM MARINE PROD.), P.O. Box 1408, Lake City, SC 29560

HEATH CO., Benton Harbor, MI 49022

IMPULSE MFG., 3343 Vincent Rd., Suite B, Pleasant Hill, CA 94523

INTRA CORP., 151 Mystic Ave., Medford, MA 02155

INMAR ELECTRONICS & SALES, 263 Washington St., Mt. Vernon, NY 10550

INT'L MARINE INSTRUMENTS, Signal Rd., Stamford, CT 06902

KENYON, New Whitfield St., Guilford, CT 06437

KING MARINE RADIO CORP., 5320 140th Ave. No., Clearwater, FL 33520

KONEL CORP., 271 Harbor Wy., S. San Francisco, CA 94080

LANGER KRELL MARINE ELECTRONICS, 526 West Ave., Miami Beach, FL 33139

LASTER INT'L, INC., 95 Madison Ave., New York, NY 10016

LAYTON INDUSTRIES, INC., 542 E. Squantum St., N. Quincy, MA 02171

LOWRANCE ELECTRONICS, INC., 12000 E. Skelly Dr., Tulsa, OK 74128

MARINE ELECTRONICS CORP., P.O. Box 1706, Lake City, SC 29560

MARINE PRODUCTS CO. (WRIGHT ELECTRONICS), P.O. Box 312, Hattiesburg, MS 39401

MARINE RECORDS CORP., P.O. Box 2001, San Diego, CA 92112

MASTER ELECTRONICS CORP., 2410 High Rd., Huntington Valley, PA 19006

MEDALLION INSTRUMENTS, 917 W. Savidge St., Spring Lake, MI 49456

MONITOR DEVICES, P.O. Box 1281, Wall, NJ 07719

MORROW ELECTRONICS, INC., P.O. Box 7078, Salem, OR 97303

NORTHSTAR MARINE PLASTIMO USA, P.O. Box 95, Redondo Bch., CA 90227

NORTHWEST INSTRUMENT, 2525 W. Commodore Way, Seattle, WA 98199

NOVA MARINE, Box 101, Ballardville, MA 01810

OSBORNE-HOFFMAN, 304 Richmond Ave., Pt. Pleasant Bch., NJ 08742

OUTBOARD MARINE CORP, Sea Horse Drive, Waukegan, IL 60085

PACE SEAMASTER, 24049 S. Frampton Ave., Harbor City, CA 90710

PARAGON ELECTRONICS, P.O. Box 1456, Bellevue, WA 98009

PATHCOM, 24049 S. Frampton Ave., Harbor City, CA 90710

PEARCE-SIMPSON, GLADDING CORP, P.O. Box 520800 GMF, Miami, FL 33152

PRESIDENT ELECTRONICS, 6345 Castleway Ct., Indianapolis, IN 46250

RACAL-DECCA MARINE, INC., P.O. Box G, Palm Coast, FL 32037

RAY JEFFERSON, Main & Cotton Sts., Philadelphia, PA 19127

RAYTHEON MARINE CO., 676 Island Pond Rd., Manchester, NH 03103

RB II, 455 Cayuga Rd., Buffalo, NY 14225

REGENCY ELECTRONICS, INC., 7707 Records St., Indianapolis, IN 46226

ROSS LABORATORIES, INC., 3138 Fairview Ave. E., Seattle, WA 98102

SEATRON MARINE ELECTRONICS, 4312 Main St., Philadelphia, PA 19127

SHAKESPEARE MARINE ELECTRONICS, 2295 NW 14th St., Miami, FL 33125

SIGNET SCIENTIFIC, 3401 Aerojet Ave., El Monte, CA 91731

SIMRAD, 1 Labriola Ct., Armonk, NY 10504

SI-TEX (SMITHS INDUSTRIES), P.O. Box 6700, Clearwater, FL 33518

SKIPPER MARINE ELECTRONICS, 3170 Commercial Ave., Northbrook, IL 60062

SONAR RADIO CORP., 3000 Stirling Rd., Hollywood, FL 33021

SOUND MARINE ELECTRONICS, 902 N.W. Leary Way, Seattle, WA 98107

SOUTHERN MARINE RESEARCH, 1401 NW 89th Ct., Miami, FL 33172

SR INSTRUMENTS, 173 Robinson St., N. Tonawanda, NY 14120

STANDARD COMMUNICATIONS, Box 92151, Los Angeles, CA 90009

TECHSONIC INDUSTRIES, One Humminbird Lane, Eufaula, AL 36027

TELCOR INSTRUMENTS, 17785 Sky Park Cir., Irvine, CA 92714

TELISONS INST. CORP., 10840 Vanowen St., N. Hollywood, CA 91605

UNIDEN CORP OF AMERICA, 19161 Triton Lane, Huntington Bch, CA 92649

UNIMETRICS MARINE PRODUCTS, 123 Jericho Turnpike, Syosset, NY 11791

VEXILAR, INC., 2850 Evans, Hollywood, FL 33020

WEBER TACKLE CO., P.O. Box 47, Stevens Point, WI 55481

WESTMAR, 905 Dester Ave. N., Seattle, WA 98109

WINDWARD MARK, 6317 Seaview Ave. NW, Seattle, WA 98107

XINTEX, 12729 Lake City Way NE, Seattle, WA 98125

Credits

Ed Wynne
cover art
design/layout/production

Aubrey Watson
photography

Frances Wynne
copy proofing

D & T Typesetting Service
Nashville, Tennessee

Lithographics, Inc.
Nashville, Tennessee
printing

Additional copies of this book available from:
Outdoor Skills Bookshelf
P.O. Box 111501
Nashville, Tennessee 37211

More fine books available from OUTDOOR SKILLS BOOKSHELF:

Buck Taylor's PRACTICAL GUIDE TO CATCHING MORE CRAPPIE. This fully-illustrated, 228-page book details exactly how and where to catch America's favorite fresh water fish *in every month of the year*! Taylor puts over 30 years of personal experience into his latest book, explaining the predictable migrations crappie make in your lake or river as seasons change, giving water depth and temperature preferences, and sharing a wealth of knowledge on techniques which fill stringers. You'll increase your catch dramatically by following the proven methods Taylor demonstrates, and you'll catch crappie *year-round* as a result! Order a copy today for only $9.95 (postpaid).

Doug Camp's TURKEY HUNTING, Spring & Fall. Camp is a professional turkey hunting guide in Alabama who can document the best client success record we have ever seen. His fully-illustrated book on turkey hunting is guaranteed to make you a better turkey hunter. Written in simple, "plain talk" terms, Camp's book covers numerous techniques for bagging a gobbler. It is a classic "How To" book on the subject, and offers you the chance to learn at the hands of a proven pro. Good reading and good information. Only $12.95 (postpaid).

Order from:

OUTDOOR SKILLS BOOKSHELF
P.O. Box 111501
Nashville, TN 37211

osb